COMBAT CAMERA

From Auntie Beeb to
the Afghan Front Line

CHRISTIAN HILL

ALMA BOOKS

ALMA BOOKS LTD
London House
243–253 Lower Mortlake Road
Richmond
Surrey TW9 2LL
United Kingdom
www.almabooks.com

First published by Alma Books Limited in 2014
Copyright © Christian Hill, 2014

Christian Hill asserts his moral right to be identified as the author of this
work in accordance with the Copyright, Designs and Patents Act 1988

Printed and bound by CPI Group (UK) Ltd, Croydon, CR0 4YY

ISBN: 978-1-84688-320-0
eBook ISBN: 978-1-84688-325-5

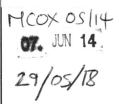

Combat Camera

To my family

COMBAT CAMERA

Author's Note

I kept a daily journal throughout my tour of Afghanistan. All the events in this book happened as described. For reasons of privacy or at their own request, the names and identifying details of some individuals have been changed.

PART ONE

The Fighting Season

At just after 7 a.m. on 19th May 2011, the Indirect Fire alarm started to sound at Camp Bastion. I heard the siren as I lay in bed, burrowing my face into my two pillows. Whenever I stayed at Bastion, I liked to make the most of its comforts – my bed also came with a duvet and a surprisingly firm, unstained mattress. Compared to life on the patrol bases, it was like staying at the Ritz.

The siren continued to wail across camp, but nobody stirred inside our air-conditioned tent. It was a drill, quite obviously. I pulled my duvet up over my head, trying to get back to the Caribbean. I'd been dreaming about an ex-girlfriend, the two of us lying on a beach in Montego Bay, such a long way from Bastion and its tedious routines.

The first explosion hit about a second later. It wasn't *that* loud, but it was still loud enough to make me jump out of bed.

"Fuck," I said.

Dougie had sprung out of his bed at the same time. He wasn't the most agile of guys, so it had to be serious.

"IDF," I heard him say, just in time for the second explosion, this one definitely closer.

I grabbed my pistol – for some reason – and ran from our tent to the Joint Media Operations Centre in my T-shirt and shorts. Dougie hurried in about ninety seconds later, fully dressed in his helmet and body armour – the correct response.

"Are we safer in here?" I asked him.

"I guess so," he said. "We should be lying on the floor, though."

We looked at each other for a long moment, two soldiers standing in a flimsy, prefabricated office. The drill in these circumstances was to lie face down on the floor with your hands by your sides, an ungainly position at the best of times. Our fear of discomfort and embarrassment outweighed any concerns about getting blown up, so we just stood there like idiots.

Faulkner walked in, the floor creaking beneath him. He was unfeasibly tall for an old pilot, and he looked even bigger in his helmet and body armour. I began to feel very underdressed.

"Christian, get round, make sure everybody is up," he said. "Helmets and body armour all round."

The all-clear siren rang out a short time later. Headquarters wasn't yielding a great deal of information about the incident – a few lines appeared on Ops Watch* at 07.40, describing "two blasts at Bastion" – but that was it. We all went off for breakfast, then returned to the office for another day of emails and phone calls, our helmets and body armour still close to hand, propped up against our desks.

Details of incidents at other Helmand bases flashed up on Ops Watch throughout the day, but we didn't realize the full scale of the offensive until Faulkner's brief in the office that evening.

"It's been one of the busiest days in Helmand for a long time," he said, a stack of printouts on his desk. "Over thirty coordinated IDF attacks on bases across the province."

He went through the details. Considering the number of incidents, the damage assessment was remarkably low.

"A couple of insurgents were killed, and some civilians died. We just had a head injury."

---

* Like a number of offices at Bastion, the JMOC had an Operations Watch terminal. A laptop hosting a near-real-time feed of incidents taking place across theatre, it reproduced reports sent directly from the field.

The attack on Bastion – the first of its kind since November 2009 – had seen two 107-mm rockets fired into the camp from rails* found seven kilometres away. One had come down on the outskirts of camp without damaging anything, while the other had landed in a vehicle yard a short walk from our office. A US Marine had to be treated for "splatter" to his back, but otherwise we were spared the casualties.

Faulkner pointed to a sketch on the whiteboard behind him. "We found another firing point with *five* rails, but all those rockets missed us." He'd drawn five lines going just wide of a blue squiggle that represented Camp Bastion. "We got lucky, to be fair. It could've been a lot worse."

I sat there listening to him, trying to remember why I'd come out here in the first place. It was a long way from the comforting world of BBC local radio, warm and fuzzy with its homely procession of shallow councillors, miserable trade unionists and confused pensioners. Quiet desperation had been enough to unseat me from my news desk in Leicester, tipping me out into the middle of the Afghan desert. Like thousands of actual proper soldiers before me, staggered throughout the last decade, I had traded boredom for potential horror. In less than a week I was due out on the first big operation of the summer, highlighting the efforts of British troops in the latest round of the war. A lot of the Taliban would get killed, and some of us would get shot and blown up too.

"If this isn't the start of the fighting season, I don't know what is," Faulkner said. "We can expect more attacks, more casualties and more vigils."

It was perfect timing for our incoming celebrity guest. The soap star turned war reporter Ross Kemp was due to land at Bastion

---

* Insurgents would fire rockets off lengths of metal rail, driven into the ground at an angle.

in a matter of hours, one of a gaggle of embeds touching down after midnight. They all had to be picked up from the flight line, briefed, accommodated and generally looked after. It was going to be a busy week for my colleagues in the office.

I met Ross the following morning. My team were filming and photographing his Tiger Aspect crew on their day-long induction package, recording for the military's archives their movements around Bastion's mock-up of an Afghan village. The mud compounds offered no respite from the heat and dust, so in between the sweaty tutorials on first aid and IED awareness, we took an early lunch in the shade of a nearby hangar. The food was standard Bastion training fare: boxes of soul-destroying sausage rolls, bags of peanuts and countless fruit-and-raisin bars.

"This food is great," said Ross, to no one in particular.

"You've obviously not tried the sausage rolls," I said.

"I like these ones." He started eating a fruit-and-raisin bar. "They're great, not like the food we had once in Musa Qala last time I was out here. We were tabbing all night, going for hours. They were dropping two-hundred-pound bombs all around us, guys were getting hit, two guys got broken legs. It was unbelievable."

He continued in this manner for another two minutes, shoving food into his mouth the whole time, telling me all about the hardships he'd faced in Musa Qala. I wasn't sure where the "two-hundred-pound bombs" had come from, but he sounded genuine enough.

"We finally got to the patrol base, just in time for breakfast, absolutely starving, and you know what they served us? One rasher of bacon and some powdered egg."

I didn't quite know how to respond to this anecdote. I had no war stories of my own, but clearly with Ross around, I didn't need any. I'd watched his DVD box set before coming out here, and seen plenty of footage of him on his hands and knees in Green Zone irrigation ditches, grimacing into the camera as the bullets whizzed overhead. That was his money shot, the reporter under fire, right in the heart of the battle. It wasn't enough for him just to interview the soldiers and tag along at the back of the patrol. He had to be seen to be in the firing line, front and centre for the ratings war.

I was different. I didn't need to crouch down in front of the camera, delivering breathless reports on the latest fighting. My presence on film was not required. I interviewed the soldiers, and I looked after my team on the ground, but that was it. My questions would always be cut from the final edit, and if I appeared in any photographs, they would always be deleted. I was the army's voiceless, invisible correspondent, right on the edge of the action, just outside the shot. Nobody wanted me in the picture, least of all my colleagues in the British media.

I left Ross to his fruit-and-raisin bars and returned to the office, where my new friend Mikkel was sitting at my desk, holding his disturbingly skull-like head in his hands, the very image of a tormented Dane.

"There has been a problem with next week's operation," he said.

I wondered for a second whether he meant the operation had been cancelled. We were supposed to be joining 1 Rifles and 42 Commando on a heli-insertion into Nahr-e Saraj. Mikkel's responsibilities extended to booking our seats on one of the helicopters. He mentored our counterparts in the newly formed Afghan Combat Camera Team. They were supposed to be joining us on the operation, learning from us, watching how it was done.

"What's wrong?" I said.

"All the helicopters are full," he said. "You'll have to go in on foot."

"Please tell me you're joking, Mikkel."

He ran a bony hand over what little remained of his hair. "At least you'll get some better footage," he said. "There'll be more action out on the ground."

This was kind of true, but it was also bullshit. The heli-insertion would've provided us with some great footage. Instead, we'd be inching our way through the IED-riddled fields of Nahr-e Saraj on foot, very probably getting shot at.

"Where are your guys going to be?" I asked him.

"I don't think they're coming."

The change of plan meant we'd now be deploying earlier than expected, flying out to Patrol Base 5 to meet up with two companies from the Afghan National Army. They were patrolling from the base via Checkpoint Sarhad to the Nahr-e Bughra canal, a distance of some three and a half kilometres. That didn't sound like much, but it would take at least two days. The plan was to clear the area of insurgents, making it safe for the Royal Engineers to build a bridge over the canal.

The plans changed again the next morning, and kept changing over the next two days. We were back on the heli-insertion, then we weren't. We were back with the Afghan National Army, then we weren't. We were driving in with the Royal Engineers on a road move, then we weren't. Tension and uncertainty ruled the day, as it always did in the run-up to an operation. Surrounded by the comforts of Bastion, we distracted ourselves as best we could, killing time in the gym and the canteen and the coffee shop.

On the night of 23rd May, I was in my tent checking over my kit – we were back on with the Afghans, flying out to Patrol Base 5 the following morning – when the news came through that a British soldier had just been seriously injured in Nahr-e Saraj. Against my better judgement, I left my kit and went over to the office to get some more details.

It was quiet that night. Only Dougie was at his desk, going through the latest field report on Ops Watch.

"Bad news," he said.

I stood behind him and read the report over his shoulder. A foot patrol out of Patrol Base 5 had struck an IED a few hundred metres from Checkpoint Sarhad. The British soldier caught in the blast had now died of his wounds. An Afghan interpreter had also been hurt – he'd been flown to Bastion with a shrapnel wound to his neck.

"Sarhad?" Dougie said. "That's where you're going, isn't it?"

"Yes," I said. "I better get back to my kit."

I left the office and went back to my tent, trying to think about my kit, trying not to think about the soldier's family back in the UK, right now being told about his death, the chaplain and the officer standing on the doorstep, heads bowed. It was the worst way to prepare for an operation, running this kind of stuff through your head, but I'd always had a stupid, flighty imagination, and I couldn't help myself. Inevitably I would start to think about my own family, my parents and my brother and my sister, all of them sitting around the dinner table at home, all of them hearing the knock at the door.

I really did not want to go on this operation. If I could've seen out the rest of my tour at Bastion, that would've suited me just fine. Yes, I'd volunteered for the Combat Camera Team, but that didn't mean I wanted to get myself killed. Like most of my career decisions to date, I didn't know what I wanted, but I knew it wasn't a grisly demise in this shithole.

I'd read enough field reports on Ops Watch to know everything I needed to know about the vast unpleasantness of combat. It was all anybody needed to know. You didn't need Ross Kemp to guide you through the horror, and you certainly didn't need the army's own-brand footage.

You just needed to read the field reports.

The Wasted Decade

I never had a burning desire to join the army – I just liked the idea of it. Notions of duty and honour appealed to the romantic idiot in me. I'd served in the cadets at school, and then the Officer Training Corps at university, so the grown-up army felt reassuringly familiar, like another warming dose of higher education. I'd graduated in the summer of 1995 with a half-baked degree in psychology, still unsure about my calling in life. I enjoyed writing, I knew that much, but that had yet to translate into an interest in journalism. Reluctant to pursue a career of any kind, I took the decision to become an army officer: my plan was to coast along on the Queen's shilling for three years, and then start worrying about a normal job.

Not unpredictably, the grown-up army put something of a rocket up my arse. Despite all my years in the cadets and the OTC, I was not prepared for Sandhurst's opening salvo of polishing, ironing and square-bashing. Throughout our first term we did nothing but drill for hours on end, marching up and down to the screams of impossible-to-please colour sergeants. At night we'd limp back to our little rooms in Old College and surrender to our wardrobes, toiling over our shirts and trousers and boots for the dreaded inspections at dawn.

It got better, thankfully. The more we learnt about soldiering, the more the colour sergeants treated us like grown-ups. We traded the Academy grounds for the great outdoors, learning how to fight in the ditches of Norfolk and the mountains of Wales. It was still difficult and unpleasant, but at least we were starting to feel like men, as opposed to errant schoolboys.

I had no desire to become a poor bloody infantryman, but I could still see the attraction in doing something toothy. When the time came to choose our regiments, I put my name down for the Royal Artillery. If I'm being honest, it was the concept of fighting at a distance that appealed to me – the idea that you could do your bit on the battlefield, but from a good ten miles away.

Happily, the Royal Artillery accepted me, so when I finally made it out of Sandhurst, I had a place waiting for me on the Young Officers' course at Larkhill. It was the home of the Royal School of Artillery, a place where second lieutenants could while away five months on a lot of cheap booze and some easygoing lessons in gunnery.

It was a wonderful period of my life, with nothing worth documenting for serious purposes – suffice to say that I was happy and content. Perhaps riding on a wave of good karma, I landed a surprise posting to one of the better Gunner units – 3rd Regiment Royal Horse Artillery.

My career at 3 RHA wasn't entirely distinguished, but then it wasn't a disaster either. It was so-so. I gained a reputation for sleeping a lot, which was understandable, given the nature of my deployments.

I spent four months in Bosnia, serving as an operations officer in a small town called Glamoč in the spring of 1999. Theoretically, it was an interesting time to be in the Balkans – NATO was attacking Belgrade, trying to stop a massacre in Kosovo – but you wouldn't have known that where we were. Glamoč was populated by Bosnian Croats, all of whom were on their best behaviour. They had no beef with NATO, naturally – we were bombing the Serbs.

I also spent six months on the Falkland Islands, working as a watch-keeper in the Joint Operations Centre near Port Stanley. The threat of invasion from Argentina was practically non-existent, so my South Atlantic campaign consisted of drinking, answering the telephone and watching movies.

* * *

By the time I left the army in January 2000, I'd decided upon a career in newspapers. I was going to study Print Journalism at City University in London for a year, then take it from there. City University had one of the best reputations for turning out journalists, so it was the natural choice. I would make myself at home in the capital, and start scribbling.

Unfortunately, when I applied to City University, they told me the Print Journalism course for that year was already fully subscribed.

"Have you thought about Broadcast Journalism?" said the quietly spoken woman on the phone. "You've got a nice voice."

What?

"Or you could wait a year."

I'd set my heart on City University – after being tied down in places like Bosnia and the Falklands, I wanted to spread my wings in London, the centre of it all. That was where all the good bars were, and that was where the media was.

I wasn't prepared to wait for a year, so I humoured the woman on the phone.

"So… Broadcast Journalism."

"Yes."

"What is it, exactly?

As she described the course to me, I suddenly saw myself in front of a camera in some distant war-torn city, telling the good people back home all about mankind's latest atrocities. I'd stay in the best bombed-out hotels and bounce back to London every weekend for champagne and sympathy.

The woman finished telling me about the prospectus, all of which had gone entirely over my head.

"OK," I said. "Put me down for that."

* * *

I went to City University, got my diploma in Broadcast Journalism and wound up getting a job at a showbiz news agency. How this tied in with my dreams of being a war reporter, I don't know, but it was work, and I needed to stay afloat. I had to travel from my tiny flat in Fulham to a grubby little office in north London every day, a journey that took more than an hour on the bus and the Tube. If that wasn't distressing enough – the whole notion of commuting was alien to me – the job itself was an even bigger shock. I was employed as an "audio editor", which involved monitoring British TV and radio stations for celebrity interviews. If someone famous popped up, I hit the record button. That was pretty much it. The only skill required was my ability to cut down the resulting audio into a showbiz news feed that was sent out to a number of European radio stations and – incredibly – Disney.

It was a shit job. I wasn't even sure it was legal. The pay was appalling and I was going nowhere fast. I couldn't even use it as a springboard into Disney. They didn't have a clue about my role. I may as well have been the caretaker.

After a fortnight, I started filling out more application forms for the BBC. This was an act of desperation. I'd already filled out a plethora at City University, and met with nothing but rejection. The BBC had one of the most time-consuming job-application forms

I'd ever seen – it was like writing a dissertation, filled with nothing but hot air. Concepts like "360-degree planning" and "holistic viewer experience" meant nothing to me, and yet I found myself writing thousands of words about them.

Then I had a break. One of our reporters managed to upset Disney with a story about George Harrison, claiming the ex-Beatle was on the verge of death. He'd recorded an interview with George Martin, attributing a number of quotes to the former Beatles manager that appeared to suggest that Harrison – stricken with cancer – only had weeks to live. The piece was bought and published by the *Mail on Sunday*, prompting a complaint from Martin. Apparently his comments had been "taken out of context", and Harrison was not as sick as the article suggested.*

With everyone at the agency terribly excited about such a big story, I'd been urged to use a couple of clips from the offending interview in my audio feed. When Disney found out we'd been responsible for upsetting George Martin – with the clips playing out on their US radio stations – they cancelled their expensive subscription to the feed with immediate effect.

Because Disney effectively bankrolled the feed, this meant I was out of a job.

Instead of making me redundant, however, the agency decided to keep me on as a reporter. This meant hanging around outside movie premieres, pestering celebrities over the phone and generally acting like a dick.

I soon decided that this was even worse than being an "audio editor". I was now an out-and-out lowlife, as opposed to one that just sat in the office all day. My days and nights were spent trying to conjure up stories that we could flog to the tabloid press. I

---

* Harrison died from lung cancer five months later.

wasn't going through anyone's rubbish bins just yet, but it was only a matter of time. The pressure was on at the agency. The economy was struggling, newspapers were struggling, and money was drying up.

We thought the Top Shop contract might turn things around. The fashion chain wanted a daily showbiz round-up for its in-store radio station. I was asked to put together a demo bulletin, voiced by myself and one of my colleagues, the soon-to-be famous Amy Winehouse. (Prior to her first record deal, she worked at the agency for about six months, although I never saw her do much reporting. She sang a lot in the office, which was nice.) We recorded a two-minute demo together, taking turns to read out the latest showbiz news, trying to pull off a winning combination of sassy and droll.

Top Shop turned us down. Our demo was sent back and tossed in the bin.

Worse was to follow, of course. Much worse.

* * *

It's difficult to write with any sensitivity about the impact of the 9/11 attacks on the entertainment-news industry, because – let's face it – no one gives a shit, but I'm going to try anyway.

Human tragedy aside, it was a disaster for the agency. The demand for celebrity bullshit disappeared overnight. It was like no one cared any more. For days after 9/11, I just sat at my desk looking at reruns of the towers collapsing. To all intents and purposes, they were a metaphor for my career as a showbiz reporter.

I got laid off a month later.

My descent into local radio began shortly after that. I loitered in Fulham for a few more months, sponging off the taxpayer, before calling it quits and returning home to Nottinghamshire. I had the basic skills needed to be a radio journalist (TV would have to wait, given the paucity of my CV), so I started applying for work-experience placements at stations across the East Midlands.

I kept banging away at the BBC – I had fantasies about landing a job at one of the big national stations, reporting to the masses – but to no avail. Eventually I got an unpaid placement at 96 Trent FM, a commercial station in Nottingham, which led to a full-time position. I did the odd reporting shift, but mainly I was used for newsreading, a pattern that was to repeat itself at several other local commercial stations for many frustrating, dispiriting years to come.

* * *

By the winter of 2008, I was still in Nottingham, stuck fast at a station called Smooth Radio. Whatever my career plan was, it had ground to a halt. I was trapped in the provinces, stretched out on the rack of commercial radio, destined to read the local news every day for the rest of my life.

It was in this spirit of self-pity that I first learnt about the Media Operations Group, or MOG. I was sitting in the newsroom, festering, waiting for my next hourly bulletin. It was already written – it only took two minutes to put together – so I turned on the TV and started watching Sky News. It was showing a report from Iraq by a soldier called Lorna Ward, a Sky journalist who was also a captain in the Territorial Army, running something called the "Combat Camera Team". I watched her creeping down a deserted street in Baghdad, clad in body armour and helmet, looking suitably anxious.

I looked up "Combat Camera Team" and found out all about the MOG. It was a TA unit based in London, always on the lookout for "media operators" with military experience – be they PR types or journalists. I took down the details.

The MOG was going to save me. There was no doubt about it.

I got a place on their selection weekend about two months later. They ran a handful every year at their Kingston upon Thames headquarters. It consisted of a series of written tests to assess our military knowledge, followed by a practical (taking questions at a mock news conference) and a couple of interviews. The Commanding Officer at the time, a blunt Ulsterman called Colonel Lucas, asked me the most important question first:

"Would you be prepared to deploy to somewhere like Afghanistan?"

"Absolutely, sir," I said, mindlessly.

I hadn't actually thought about the reality of an operational tour in Afghanistan. If Colonel Lucas had asked me to stick my head in a lion's mouth, I would have given him exactly the same answer. I was desperate to make something happen with my life – my career was dying. I knew that if I was going to deploy to Afghanistan, they would want me for the Combat Camera Team – "news-gatherers" were in short supply in the MOG – but I hadn't even begun to consider the risks involved. My priority was to get through the selection weekend – I would worry about everything else later.

Four days later I got a letter in the post, welcoming me into the MOG.

* * *

I didn't volunteer for Afghanistan straight away. I wasn't a complete idiot. I needed some time to feel my way back into the military. Just becoming a reservist was strange enough. As a regular, I'd always been a bit sniffy about the TA – surely the army was a lifestyle choice rather than a weekend pursuit? How could you commit to a role that might require you to sacrifice your life, when you were doing something else five days a week?

I soon got over my prejudices. I was no longer some tragic underachiever in his mid-thirties who read the news for peanuts on local radio. Those days were over. I was now a part-time army officer in his mid-thirties who read the news for peanuts on local radio. In my mind, there was a huge difference. There was now a light at the end of the tunnel; I could see some sort of career path emerging. I didn't know whether it would lead to Afghanistan necessarily, but at this stage I didn't care. I was just glad to have some of my self-respect back.

I got laid off three months later. The station was merging with its sister site in Birmingham. There were three of us working in the newsroom in Nottingham, and one of us had to go. Unable to muster the enthusiasm needed to preserve my role, I got the P45.

I applied for a vacant position in the newsroom at BBC Radio Leicester, but it meant nothing. I was washing my hands of local radio. I'd spent most of the decade in that particular rut and now I wanted out. It was time to do something with my life, even if it meant possibly losing it. The MOG was always on the lookout for the next Combat Camera Team leader, so getting a tour lined up would not be a problem. The BBC application was just a token gesture, intended to fail, intended to hasten my lurch towards Afghanistan. I filled out the form during the last few days of my Smooth Radio notice period, killing time between bulletins. If I had any last-second doubts about volunteering for the Combat Camera Team, I could always tell myself that I'd tried – and failed – to find a normal job.

BBC HR got back to me a week later, just as I was girding my loins to make the big call to the MOG. Apparently, the Managing Editor at BBC Radio Leicester had been impressed with my application form. Was I available for an interview?

The BBC dream was still alive, it seemed. Without getting too carried away, I started to wonder whether a spell at BBC Radio Leicester might not in fact be a good idea. With my nose in the Corporation trough, I'd be in a decent position to sniff out a job at one of the national stations, broadcasting to the masses. I'd spent almost ten years in the hinterlands of local radio, fantasizing about a role in one of the newsrooms at Broadcasting House. Surely it was worth giving it one last shot, before riding off into the Afghan sunset?

* * *

I put the call to the MOG on hold, went to the interview at BBC Radio Leicester – and got the job. At the time, I thought the planets must have aligned. Only later did I learn that the Managing Editor – a bohemian turned journalist called Kate Squire – was specifically looking for a decent newsreader. The interview had gone quite badly, in fact. I had no idea, for instance, that so much emphasis would be placed on their *Breakfast Show*.

"Tell us about our *Breakfast Show* this morning," Kate had said. "What did you like about it, and what would you have done to improve it?"

"I'm afraid I was quite busy this morning," I said casually. "I didn't get a chance to listen to it."

I've since learnt that this sort of response is normally enough to derail a BBC interview completely, but obviously the newsreading gods (and Kate) were smiling on me, and my slip-up was overlooked.

I enjoyed working at BBC Radio Leicester – my colleagues in the newsroom were a good crowd, and made me feel more than welcome – but it was always just a means to an end. I read the bulletins on the *Breakfast Show* for six months, familiarizing myself with the BBC way of doing things, and then I applied for a placement at one of the national stations. The man I had to impress was a newsreader himself, a minor celebrity called Alan Dedicoat (aka the "Voice of the Balls" on the National Lottery). He oversaw the BBC's top stable of radio newsreaders, and had the power to lever me into one of the national slots for a trial run. If he liked my voice, I could be reading on BBC Radio Two within days. If not, I was going nowhere. I emailed him a demo bulletin on 7th July 2010 and awaited his reply.

He got back in touch a few days later with the following email:

Good morning!

Well, I've taken a listen... and sadly, it's not quite what I'm after.

– It's a bit "sung" for my liking

– And breathy in places

– Each story's read in exactly the same way

– There's virtually no attack at the start of each item; there's nothing to make me listen up

– Frankly, it sounds a bit like you're more concerned with how you sound than what you're reading

– How high's the volume on your headphones?

Sorry, but you did ask!

I was a little taken aback by this – I didn't agree with any of his points – but at least he wasn't sugar-coating it. I replied to that effect:

OK Alan, thanks for the honesty!

There wasn't much else I could say. I was in no position to start arguing with him. He probably got dozens of demos from BBC staffers like me every week.

He replied five minutes later:

Well, it's not a write-off, Christian – don't think that. I'm just looking for something special. Listeners have just one shot at understanding the news. They don't have the script or prior knowledge of the stories. We're honour-bound to help them understand FIRST TIME. We shouldn't "colour" it with the way we sound or how we say things.

My real problem is everyone wants to join us.

If you're in town at all, call me and take me for coffee!

Of course I was never going to call him and take him for coffee. Perhaps I could've sent him another demo in six months, or approached somebody else of equal standing, but I just didn't have the energy. Trying to crack Broadcasting House could take years, and what would I be doing in the meantime? The prospect of more local radio, decades of it, stretched out before me like a desolate plain, too depressing to contemplate.

I was a desperate journeyman, looking for a seismic shift, something to break up the long, unwanted trek. I needed a fault line to open up, something that would reveal a deeper, more precious route. Something quicker, riskier and with greater reward.

I wasn't about to leave the BBC altogether – that was my safety line. A brief descent was all that was required, then I'd haul myself back up to the surface, hopefully in a new and magical land.

As long as the ground didn't swallow me whole, I'd be just fine.

Home Fires

Telling your family you've volunteered to go to Afghanistan is never an easy thing. Why would anybody in their right mind want to go there? Even if you don't mention the war, it's a tough sell. It's the poorest country in Asia, it generates most of the planet's heroin and it's stupidly hot. Throw in the firefights, the IEDs and the suicide bombers, and you've got that most difficult of pitches: "Hell on Earth".

With no wife or girlfriend to speak of – my love life to that point had been a series of mildly amusing disasters, worthy of their own comic novella – I only had to worry about breaking the news to my parents. I did also have a brother and sister, but they were much less of a concern: both Will and Nicky took after our father's side of the family, being typically English and phlegmatic about things like love and war. Unlike myself, they shared none of our mother's Germanic fondness for tearful sentimentality.

I told my parents on a frosty evening just a few days before Christmas, stopping by on my way home from work. My mother was standing by the fire in the lounge when I broke the news, while my father was in his favourite chair, reading his newspaper.

"I've got something important to tell you," I said.

I wasn't normally given to statements like this. Already my mother looked worried. My father put his paper down.

"I'm going to Afghanistan."

My mother's face dropped, and she started to cry.

Shit.

What was I doing, putting her through this? She didn't deserve this. She'd brought me into this world, loved me and looked after me. Now I was dropping this on her.

"How long for?" she said eventually.

"Four months."

More tears. I think that for a second she'd been hoping it might have been some short journalistic assignment, lasting just a few days or weeks. The fact was, it could've been worse – it could've been six months. I'd requested a shorter tour, and luckily I'd got it.

"Are they making you go?" asked my father. He wasn't crying, but he did have his "serious" face on, eyeing me carefully over the top of his reading glasses.

"They asked me if I wanted to go, and I said I did." This was sort of true, insofar as the MOG was always asking for volunteers. "I think it'll be good for me."

"What will you be doing?" my mother asked.

"I'll be running a camera team." Already I was omitting the word "combat". "There'll be myself, a cameraman and a photographer."

"Will it be dangerous?"

I considered telling an outright lie to this question, claiming my job was entirely office-bound, but I wasn't sure it would wash. My mother was pretty good at detecting bullshit; if she thought I was trying to protect her from the truth, it could make things even worse.

"It shouldn't be too bad," I said. "We might have to go out on the odd patrol."

She looked unconvinced, her cheeks still wet with tears. I gave her a hug.

"It's going to be OK," I said. "If it was that dangerous, I wouldn't be doing it."

To be honest, I had no idea how dangerous it was going to be. I only knew that I didn't want to get hurt. If the Taliban had seen fit to publish a "Forecast of Events", then maybe I could've made an informed decision. Sadly, they had no media planner to keep us journalists informed about their future movements. They just did what they did on a seemingly random basis, attacking coalition troops whenever it took their fancy, terrorizing all our mothers in the process.

* * *

My colleagues at BBC Radio Leicester reacted to the news of my departure in a slightly different manner to that of my mother. They threw me a leaving party at a lap-dancing club. Remarkably, all the girls in the newsroom came as well. I think they looked upon the excursion as a kind of anthropological field trip, an opportunity to peer under the rock where drunk and/or lonely men go to stare at naked women.

I enjoyed it, anyway. We all drank an incredible amount of vodka, then everyone chipped in for a lap dance, buying me ten minutes with a peroxide blonde who'd squeezed herself and her Hindenburg breasts into a Stars and Stripes Lycra dress. I had just a short moment to contemplate the significance of our special relationship with the US, then the dress came off and the Hindenburgs were in my face, threatening to crash-land onto my forehead before veering back up again, floating around in a dreamlike sequence that was over all too quickly.

Two days later I started my pre-deployment training at Chetwynd Barracks in Chilwell, just down the road from my home. My hangover had just about cleared by then, so I was ready for all the inglorious demands of mobilization: filling in forms, pissing into test tubes, getting injected, practising battlefield casualty drills and shooting on the range in the freezing January rain. I was a full-time soldier again, on the regular payroll until my scheduled return to BBC Radio Leicester in September. It felt good – the pay was much better, and there was plenty of leave to look forward to, in between all the military stuff. I had a sporadic timetable of training up until mid-March, then I'd fly out and do my thing in the desert for four months, before flying back in time for the tail end of the English summer. Already I was imagining myself in my garden, sitting on the patio in the undemanding August sunlight, sipping a gin-and-tonic, the war safely behind me.

Some volunteer for war because they want to fight, and some volunteer because they want to come back. No prizes for guessing which group I belonged to.

I had a lot of time to prepare for my deployment on 10th March, but in the end it all turned into a mad rush. I left my packing until the last day, which is never a good idea. By the time I'd stuffed all my kit into my issued black holdall and my Bergen rucksack, there was barely any room left for personal items. Even the books I was hoping to take had to stay behind. I made a desperate last-minute attempt to force *Memoirs of an Infantry Officer* by Siegfried Sassoon into the holdall, but it refused to go.

My woeful lack of personal organization meant there was little time for goodbyes, which was probably a blessing. I bolted down a final meal at my parents' house – beef stir fry, a favourite of mine – before giving my teary-eyed mother a farewell hug, promising I would "keep my head down". The two dogs, Monty and Trudie, got a quick pat and a scratch, then I had to go.

My father gave me a lift to Chetwynd Barracks, where I had to pick up my rifle and pistol before taking the military transport down to Brize Norton. We didn't say much on the way there: we just listened to the radio, making occasional small talk. Neither of us had any desire to chat about Afghanistan, but what else was there?

Only when we were saying goodbye did my father give me some advice. He parked outside the armoury at Chetwynd Barracks, helped me with my bags, then shook my hand and hugged me.

"Look after number one," he said.

Look after number one. It was pretty good advice, to be fair. Probably some of the best he's ever given me.

Unfortunately, I wasn't really in a position to follow it.

The Combat Camera Team

I'd arranged to meet up with my cameraman Russ and my photographer Ali later that evening. The two of them were making their own way to Brize Norton from their homes in Devon and the West Midlands. Our flight wasn't due to leave until seven o'clock the following morning, so there was no rush. In keeping with the military's favourite dictum – "hurry up and wait" – we'd been told to get to the airport the night before.

Having said goodbye to my father, I drew my SA80 rifle and Browning pistol from the armoury, then installed myself in the back of the "military transport" – a white minibus – with the rest of my kit. The only other passenger was a young signaller who was listening to his iPod and gazing out of the window. We had a two-hour drive to Brize Norton ahead of us, with a restless night in the airport's transit accommodation to come. I fashioned a pillow from my spare combat jacket and tried to get some sleep.

As it turned out, the journey to Brize Norton took little more than ninety minutes. Our driver, a deeply suntanned corporal, completed it in record time, ruling out any possibility of sleep.

"I've had to cancel an hour with a prostitute in Mansfield to take you two," he complained at one point, his foot hard on the accelerator. The whole minibus was shaking. I looked over his shoulder at the speedometer – we were doing ninety miles an hour.

I thought about telling him to slow down, then decided not to bother. What was the point? Far greater dangers lay ahead of me, so it was probably a good idea to start getting comfortable with the whole concept of death. If I couldn't overcome my fears in a speeding minibus on the M1, what chance did I have in Afghanistan?

"I normally do the pick-ups," he said. "I get to see you guys come off the plane, your eyes full of trauma." He chuckled. "From all the horrors you've seen."

I looked across at the signaller. Thankfully, he was still staring out of the window, lost in the sounds of his iPod.

"Don't worry, it's not as bad as you think." The corporal was looking back at me now, still doing 90 mph. "I've done two tours myself. You'll be OK."

Strangely, I started worrying about getting killed in four months' time, on the return journey. What if this guy was driving me then? Dying on the way to Afghanistan didn't seem so bad, but getting killed on the way back, in a minibus with this clown, seemed unbearably tragic.

We managed to get to Brize Norton without incident. The corporal dropped us off outside the main entrance to the Departures terminal, wishing us a safe tour before he left.

"See you in four months, sir."

"Well, yes," I said, unenthusiastically.

I loaded my kit onto a luggage trolley – just like I was going on holiday – and made my way into the near-empty terminal. I had been expecting to find hundreds of soldiers milling about, but there was just one shaven-headed sergeant, fast asleep across a row of seats, oblivious to the BBC News 24 headlines pumping out of the large television above him. I handed over my baggage and weapons to a bored-looking woman on the check-in desk, just as the newsreader announced that another soldier had been killed in Afghanistan.

I parted company with the signaller, wishing him a safe tour ("Have a safe tour" was practically a mantra) before heading over to the bar. Like the main terminal, it was virtually deserted. Russ and Ali were sitting on a sofa in the corner, watching television. They stood up when I walked in, and we exchanged handshakes and greetings.

"Hi boss," they both said.

I'd met the two of them for the first time on a week-long Combat Camera Team course a month earlier. Within hours they'd taken to calling me "boss" rather than "sir", a more informal term of address which I didn't mind in the least. Despite all my pre-deployment training, I still saw myself as a civilian who was being allowed to wear a military uniform and go on an awfully big adventure. Most of my standing as "the boss" came from my BBC credentials: my military experience, ranked alongside that of Russ and Ali, was pretty limited.

"What are you drinking?" I asked them.

Ali had a glass of red wine, while Russ opted for a pint. We stood at the empty bar, chatting about potential stories, the two of them sipping at their drinks like a pair of designated drivers, clearly intent on an early night. Keen to set the right example, I followed suit, nursing my pint like an alcoholic who knows he's not going to have another beer for four months.

One of the possible stories we discussed was a profile on Ali herself trying her hand as a war photographer. Ordinarily she worked as a civilian freelancer, photographing all manner of domestic stories for the British press. She'd only just signed up for the Media Operations Group a few months earlier, having previously completed twelve years' service in the regulars, joining the RAF as a policewoman in 1995. She didn't look like someone who could wrestle a drunken pilot to the ground and slap on the cuffs – she was only about 5'5" – but she was a tough character nonetheless, and could draw on a lot of operational experience, having served in Northern Ireland, Bosnia and Iraq.

Russ had also seen a fair bit of the world. Unlike Ali and me, he was a serving soldier, based in the Media and Communications team at the British Army's headquarters in Andover. He'd joined the army in 1994, serving as a tank mechanic in the Royal Electrical and Mechanical Engineers (REME) for ten years, before transferring into the Royal Logistics Corps to become a photographer (the RLC ran the army's stable of photographers) and then a cameraman. He'd already completed two short tours of Afghanistan, and had previously served in Iraq and Kosovo.

We discussed a couple of other potential stories – sniffer dogs, Afghan pilots – then made our way over to the transit accommodation. It was quite civilized, as it turned out, each of us getting our own room. I thought that maybe I would get a reasonable amount of sleep, but in the end I lay awake in my single bed for over an hour, thinking about Russ and Ali, and whether I was the right man to lead them.

It was better than worrying about getting blown up, I guess.

I managed to get about four hours' sleep before a woman's voice, piped into my room through a speaker over my bed, informed me that it was 03.15, which meant that it was time to get up. They didn't like oversleepers here, for obvious reasons. I shaved and dressed, and then made my way over to the canteen. It was full of soldiers, but the atmosphere was subdued. I made small talk with Russ and Ali while we ate our cereal and toast. They were both pretty quiet too.

After breakfast we all sat in the Departures terminal for two and a half hours. We were finally herded onto our Tristar at 06.30. It felt crowded on board – the flight was almost fully booked, and we all had to carry on our helmets and flak jackets – but the three of us managed to get a row of seats together, with Russ in the middle.

The eight-hour flight went fairly quickly, broken up by a stopover in Akrotiri. Ali spent most of the time reading on her Kindle, while Russ played his favourite video game, *Angry Birds*. Despite being in his early thirties, I'd noticed that his cultural preferences tended towards the adolescent: he was a big fan of *Star Wars*, and he couldn't get enough of conspiracy theories. After he'd managed to complete an *Angry Birds* level (whatever that involved), he talked to me at some length about the Apollo moon landings.

"There are no stars in the pictures," he said. "Those photographs were taken in a studio at Area 51."

I thought he was talking rubbish, but I humoured him, keen to hear his so-called evidence.

"They were using Hasselblad cameras. Why would they use Hasselblad cameras? You'd never take them up to the moon with you."

"Why not?" I'd never heard of Hasselblad cameras.

"They're difficult to use. They had no viewfinders. They couldn't have produced all those photos."

Russ continued in this vein for some time, all of his evidence coming back to the photographs. I wasn't in the least bit convinced by his argument, but it did make me realize how much he loved photography. I knew he could handle his P2 video camera, but I was beginning to suspect he'd much rather have Ali's Nikon D3S in his hands instead.

He went back to his *Angry Birds*, while I mulled over the apparent lure of photography over moving imagery. Plainly, stills came with a sense of authorship that was often lacking in video footage.

Russ's output, when broadcast on national television, would be cut from his rushes by various editors and come with a little caption saying "MoD Footage". Ali's work, on the other hand, would appear untouched in national papers with her name credited right underneath. Every generation produces a handful of famous war photographers, but cameramen in conflicts go largely unknown.

Both Russ and Ali wanted to be recognized as talented individuals, which sounded great, but had the potential to cause me a few problems. I was supposed to be steering their material in the general direction of our key messages: we were in the process of handing over to the Afghan forces, we were helping to rebuild the country, things were getting better, we'd soon be out of here. We were content providers for the military's Media Operations machine, producing footage and imagery that served the interests of the British mission in Afghanistan. To that end, the message took precedence over the execution. Naturally we had to distribute a quality product, otherwise no media outlets would touch it, but there was no point marketing something that failed to support our messages. That didn't always sit easily with individual expression, and certain journalistic tendencies would have to be kept in check until our return.

We entered Afghan airspace about half an hour before we were due to land. The pilot switched off the cabin lights and told us to put on our helmets and flak jackets. We sat in silence, all of us alone in our thoughts, the silhouettes of our helmets making us look like rows of mushrooms in the half-darkness.

I couldn't help but think of the old line about soldiers and mushrooms being kept in the dark and fed on shit. This was slightly different, however, in that I found myself wondering whether I'd be doing any of the shit-feeding myself.

PART TWO

Inside the Wire

Camp Bastion rose out of the wastes of the Afghan desert like a mirage, rich with the promise of doughnuts and air-conditioning. The size of Reading, its sprawling arrangement of tents, offices and hangars catered to the needs of thousands of British and American troops. Canteens as big as warehouses kept us fed and watered, chilly gymnasiums with long rows of cardiovascular machines kept us fit, and Portakabin ablution blocks with priceless hot showers kept us clean. Save for the occasional sandstorm, you could've seen out a six-month tour here and not even known you were in the desert. Generators across the camp chugged and hummed in a pleasing, reassuring manner, bringing us two of the essentials for a stress-free military occupation: electricity and climate control. Had the Taliban worked out a way to knock out our power supply, we'd have left this sun-ruined part of the world years ago – but they hadn't, so we were sticking around for a bit.

In the heart of this temporary but probably permanent monument to Western overstretch was the JMOC, my official base for the next four months. My colleagues and I lived out of two six-man tents, our "rooms" divided by sheets that hung all the way down from the canvas ceiling to the plastic matting on the floor. Privacy of any kind was a rare operational commodity, so this was indeed a privileged arrangement, although you couldn't so much as scratch your balls without someone hearing you.

There was a third tent, just for the visiting media. It sat between the two staff tents, doubling as an office for the journalists. A trestle table surrounded by fold-up chairs took up one half of the tent, while ten bunk beds crowded up the other half. When it was full, it was unbearable – even the most docile battery hens would've struggled to get a good night's sleep in there – but that was entirely the point. We didn't want anyone from the media getting too comfortable right on our doorstep.

Less than ten yards from our tents was the JMOC itself. A glorified Portakabin, it housed an open-plan office with half a dozen desks, each boasting a telephone and a computer. A flatscreen television hung in the centre of the far wall, invariably tuned to one of the rolling news channels. Beneath it a printer churned out the latest Afghan-related headlines from the newspapers back home – they were sourced online and stuck to a cuttings board by the door. The rest of the wall space was given over to a spread of maps, whiteboards and day planners, all of them daubed in black and blue non-permanent scribble. Cables ran across the floor from every corner of the room, stuck down with lengths of gaffer tape. A clutch of them ran through the near wall and out onto a gravel pathway to our very own disproportionately large satellite dish, covered in dust and pointing towards the heavens, reminding us all that Bastion really was in the middle of nowhere.

As with most offices at Bastion, the JMOC had a tendency to induce cabin fever. The camp was an incredibly safe place – probably the safest place in Afghanistan – and if you were trapped inside its sterile confines for any length of time, you got restless. Some officers, wedged behind a desk for six months, found themselves clawing at the walls. They volunteered for all kinds of unnecessary tasks, loath to go home without at least a sniff of the Green Zone.

Bored stupid, they talked about going outside the wire like it was some sort of robust leisure activity.

Harriet was not one of them. Pink-faced and bespectacled, she was our media planner, handling the timetables for my team and the various embedded reporters who passed through Bastion. Apart from making the odd trip to the flight line, ferrying journalists in the JMOC minibus, she spent all of her time in the office, writing emails and making phone calls. She had no desire to go outside the wire. She was a quietly spoken RAF reservist who loved sudoku. The thought of going out on a Helmand safari almost certainly terrified her, but she had the good sense to keep those fears to herself.

Our boss was a very different creature. Wing Commander Faulkner's military record spoke for itself: as a Hercules pilot, he'd flown countless operational missions in numerous hotspots around the world. Hitting his fifties, his flying days behind him, he'd transferred into the cosseted world of Media Operations. He wanted to go on safari, absolutely, but he also had a talent for sitting in the JMOC chasing bullshit.

"You'll be going out quite a bit," he told me on my first day, the two of us standing outside the office in the sunshine. "Make sure you sit down with Harriet and get your timetable sorted out."

"How's it been going so far, sir?" Along with Harriet, he'd already been in theatre for two months.

"It's been quiet," he said. "But I've managed to get outside the wire a couple of times, which helps."

I nodded. He clearly subscribed to the "get outside the wire, it'll do you good" school of thought.

"Harriet has yet to go outside," he added, smiling. "But I'm hoping to change that."

Poor old Harriet. She was sitting inside the cool office, picking her way through her emails, blissfully unaware of our conversation. I tried to picture her in the middle of the Green Zone, picking her way through a field of IEDs, trying not to collapse in the life-threatening heat.

It was difficult to imagine, to be honest.

Later that afternoon, a handful of young soldiers from the nearby REME battalion trudged over to the JMOC for some interview training. They were about to complete their six-month tour and were due to be interviewed by the local media at their homecoming parade back in the UK. Their commanding officer had chosen them in the hope they would come across well on camera, but to a man they all looked pasty and miserable.

"Try to look happier," I told them, then immediately regretted it. Maybe one of their colleagues had died?

"It's just been a bit boring," one of them said. "We haven't been outside the wire once."

Maybe Faulkner had a point after all.

* * *

During our first week at Bastion, we had to complete a training package called Reception Staging and Onward Integration (RSOI). Every morning at sunrise about a hundred of us caught a fleet of buses to the desolate outskirts of the base, where the training took place in a series of tents and purpose-built compounds.* Most of it was revision, repeating the lessons we'd spent the last two months learning back in the UK. If you were staying inside the wire for the duration of your tour, you only had to complete a two-day package, but for those going out on the ground, a minimum of five days

---

* Also known as the Afghan training village.

was needed. Counter-IED drills took up most of the timetable, along with first aid, all of it ramming home the blunt message: *If you don't do your drills properly, this is what could happen to you.* We were shown graphic slides of double amputees and triple amputees fresh off the battlefield, their limbs reduced to bloated, crimson stumps. Our instructors even showed us close-up pictures of IED victims who'd been wearing pelvic protection alongside those who hadn't.

But the most memorable lesson, if "memorable" is the right word, was a talk by a skinny, unshaven corporal from the Royal Irish Regiment, days away from the end of his tour. He gave us a presentation called "Theatre Realities" inside a tent filled with nothing but wooden benches. There were no maps and no graphic slides – it was just him standing there, describing his experiences over the past six months. We sat down on the benches and listened to his lilting Irish accent for almost an hour, none of us making a sound.

He started by talking about Ranger Steven McKee, a colleague who had been killed by an IED in Nad-e Ali just a week earlier.

"I was with Stevie on the day he died," he said. "He was driving a Jackal. We'd been going across this wadi all day, with no problems. He drew his vehicle alongside mine for a brief, then drove off and, about thirty metres later, he hit the IED.

"Stevie had no chance. It took off the whole of the front of the Jackal. The top-cover man got blown onto the back of the vehicle – he got broken limbs and a burst eardrum. Miraculously, the vehicle commander just got a cut on his forehead. He got out and staggered back towards us. How he managed to walk away from it, we don't know."

I glanced at some of the faces around me. Everyone was rapt, hanging on the corporal's every word.

"Multiple firing points have become a growing problem," he continued. "One of our patrols went out, and they got hit from eight different points. The lead man got hit in the buttock with an armour-piercing round which exited through the front of his thigh, blowing most of it away. The fire was still coming in, so his patrol commander told him to roll into an irrigation ditch, which he did. Unfortunately, the ditch had five feet of water in it, so now he was drowning. The patrol medic then sprinted across, swallow-dived into the ditch, and saved the guy's life.

"In another incident," he went on, "some of our guys came under fire, and they all jumped into a ditch for cover. One of the insurgents ran around to the end of ditch and shot down the entire length of it. Luckily, because they were staggered, he missed all of them, apart from the guys on each end who were both hit on their side-plates."

The stories kept coming, one after the other. It was almost hypnotic, the way he spoke.

"Your pelvic protection can make a big difference," he said, still going. "We had a guy from the Engineers who lost both his legs and an arm in an IED blast. First thing he said when he came round was 'Have I still got my cock and balls?' Fortunately, he was wearing his pelvic protection, and it did the job."

After the talk, we all shuffled out of the tent and collected our packed lunches. Everyone was pensive, examining the colourless sausage rolls in silence. Many of us, I suspect, were quietly recalculating the odds of getting out of this country in one piece.

We had another Theatre Realities talk the following afternoon. This one was a bit more upbeat. A surprisingly portly captain from the Mercians stood in front of us and did his best to lift the mood.

"You hear a lot of doom and gloom about Afghanistan, but actually it's not so bad," he said. "It's ninety per cent boredom, really, and only ten per cent shitting yourself."

* * *

One of our first proper jobs on camp was at the hospital, highlighting the quality of emergency care for injured troops. We'd arranged to film and interview a batch of TA medics for ITV Yorkshire. Russ and I were able to walk there from the JMOC – it was only four hundred yards away, just behind Pizza Hut and the Heroes coffee bar.

It wasn't the biggest hospital I'd ever seen, but it was one of the busiest. The single-storey building contained eight trauma-resuscitation bays, four operating tables, eleven intensive-care beds and thirty-five intermediate-care beds. Almost two hundred staff ran the wards, most of them from 212 (Yorkshire) Field Hospital, a TA unit based in Sheffield. British and US helicopters kept them supplied with patients around the clock, using a helipad a short drive from the Emergency Department. They dealt with up to thirty cases of battle trauma a day, ranging from gunshot wounds to multiple amputations.

We'd only just got there when the MERT* landed with a casualty: an Afghan soldier shot in the abdomen. He was stretchered from the Chinook into the back of a waiting ambulance, which

---

*   The British-run Medical Emergency Response Team – or MERT – consisted of a doctor, two paramedics and an emergency nurse, along with a protection force of four soldiers, deploying in a Chinook helicopter. The US ran smaller medevac teams in Pave Hawk helicopters under the call sign Pedro.

sped from the helipad to the Emergency Department in less than a minute. The hospital staff then took over, carrying him into a vacant trauma bay, preparing him for surgery. Russ filmed the trauma team in action, careful to avoid shots of the Afghan's face (there being strict rules on patient confidentiality). The wound was relatively straightforward – the bullet had exited through his buttock. The team cleaned him up, and he was wheeled into the operating theatre.

Russ and I followed him into theatre, but kept our distance during the surgery. Once he had been stabilized, we did a quick interview with one of the surgeons, a colonel in her fifties from Rotherham. She chatted away happily, answering all my undemanding questions, while the Afghan was stitched up in the background.

We managed a couple more interviews – with a nurse and a ward supervisor – before word came through that the MERT was on its way back again with another casualty. This time it was a Brit, and it was serious.

"IED," said one of the medics. "Triple amp."

We decided to stop filming. At least a dozen extra staff – most of them junior medics – had gathered around the trauma bay just to watch the casualty being brought in. It was crowded, much more crowded than it needed to be. Russ switched off the camera and we went for a coffee, walking over to Heroes without saying a word.

What was more important? Preserving the dignity of a single soldier or showcasing the grisly consequences of an IED blast? At the time, it felt like the right thing to do, the decent thing to do, not to loom over a raw triple amputee. We didn't need to film him – we already had enough coverage of the trauma team in action – and the footage would've been far too graphic for a normal audience.

For the younger medics crowding around his bed, it was very different. By their own admission, they took in the gore whenever they could: it was part education and part desensitization. They were in the business of acting humanely, but first of all they had to detach some of that humanity from themselves and the casualty. Many of them likened themselves to mechanics, putting the various pieces of the human machine back together as best they could. It was part of their coping strategy, allowing them to function without the burden of messy emotions.

Maybe, like the medics, I should've tried to desensitize myself. For a long time afterwards I wondered whether we should've stayed in that trauma bay and kept filming. Even if it was too much for ITV Yorkshire – and even if it was too much *for him*, served up on film like a piece of meat – the footage could've still been used by some other media outlet, somewhere along the line. Maybe in a documentary, or even just a training video.

I didn't say much in Heroes. Neither did Russ. We just drank our coffee and watched the RAF bomb Libya on Sky News. The rolling news channels had been all over the air campaign against Colonel Qadafi's regime for the last week. Wherever the bombs were falling, the whole world would know about it. There was no word yet on the exact number of casualties, but none of them were British.

Back in the JMOC I checked Ops Watch for more details on the triple amputee. He'd been on a foot patrol with 2 Para in Nahr-e Saraj. Initial reports suggested he was a member of a counter-IED team from Brimstone, a call sign made up of bomb-disposal experts and searchers who went out looking for the devices ahead of the main body of troops. He'd triggered an IED thought to contain around five kilograms of explosives. This was at the lower end of the scale for the Taliban, but it was still powerful enough to blow away both of his legs and one of his arms.

He hadn't died though, so aside from family and friends, no one back home would know that a British soldier had just lost three of his limbs. The JMOC wasn't about to trumpet the news, and neither was the British media. If you wanted to make a name for yourself out here, you had to go the whole hog and get yourself killed.

The injuries kept coming, and you took it for granted that someone somewhere was about to get blown up. The next morning another British soldier stepped on an IED, also in Nahr-e Saraj. He was more fortunate, losing just a leg below the knee. Traumatic amputations were so common in Helmand, so unremarkable, they never made the news. They were simply a part of the Afghan landscape, undeserving of a headline.

Shahzad

Our first job outside the wire was with 3 Para in Nad-e Ali, two weeks into our tour. BBC Four had requested footage of the Paras in Afghanistan to use in their documentary series *Regimental Stories*, which focused on different units within the British Army, looking at their history, training and current deployments. We were flying out to 3 Para's headquarters at Patrol Base Shahzad, driving out to one of their smaller bases, then going out on foot with one of their patrols. Ali was also coming, taking photographs that would hopefully be of interest to the British press.

Before we left Bastion I stopped by the office to say goodbye to Sean, the outgoing Combat Camera Team leader who was about to catch his flight home. A wiry ex-Marine in his late twenties, he'd been full of advice during his handover to me, some of it useful, some of it less so. When he wasn't in uniform, he worked for a shipping firm in Glasgow. How this qualified him for a position in Media Operations, I had no idea, but he seemed to like it out here.

"So you all set for Nad-e Ali?" he said.

"I think so."

"Make sure you put one of your dog tags in your boot."

"Why?" Both of my identity discs were hanging around my neck.

"In case your legs get blown off."

"Seriously?"

He looked at me sympathetically. I felt a story coming on. Like Afghanistan itself, Sean was full of them. You never had to look far to find something dramatic out here, and if Media Operations was your line of work, you were in clover. It was just a case of weeding out all the nasty stuff before you got to the telling.

"I was on this patrol last month," Sean began. "We came across this compound, and were about to go in and take a look around, when a friendly Afghan ran across and told us not to go in, because it was littered with IEDs. So we didn't go in, we carried on our way. But as we were walking past one of the open doorways, we saw a soldier's boot just lying there, still with the foot inside."

It wasn't the most reassuring story I'd ever heard. Sean needed to work on his editing skills, clearly.

"It's not uncommon to see lumps of flesh just rotting by the side of the track," he added. "Sometimes it's not worth the risk, clearing it up."

"Sounds wonderful, Sean."

He smiled. "Don't worry, Julian, you'll be fine."

"*Julian*?" I said. "It's Christian."

"Christian?"

"Yes, *Christian*."

It had seemed like a genuine mistake on Sean's part, getting my name wrong, but it spooked me nonetheless. Julian was a fellow member of the MOG, and to my knowledge the only Combat Camera Team leader to have come to any harm out here. It had happened a year earlier. He'd been hit by shrapnel, a blast fragment skewering his hand while he was out with his cameraman.

"I'm not great with names," Sean said. "Sorry about that."

Julian had recovered OK, but it wasn't exactly a good omen. I was feeling uneasy as it was – two Irish Guards had just been killed by an IED in the last week of their tour, and a Para who'd lost his legs a few days earlier had also just died. There was a lot of death going on, and it was still only March.

Sean then made matters worse by showing me a clip from his head cam of an IED blowing up four soldiers on a joint patrol earlier in his tour.

"I don't want to shit you up," he said, opening the file on his laptop. "But I think you should see what an IED blast looks like."

The clip began with Sean at the back of the patrol, walking along a wide, sandy track with his cameraman a few yards in front of him. A line of about a dozen Afghan soldiers stretched out ahead of them, leading to the corner of a mud compound seventy yards away. The point man had stopped just short of it and was pondering his next move, the corners of walls being known as hotspots for IEDs. A moment later he stepped off the track and continued with the patrol, putting some extra space between himself and the wall, the soldiers behind him following in his footsteps.

He'd only gone a few yards when the IED – buried near the foot of the wall – exploded. Sean and everybody else froze, the head cam trained on a huge cloud of smoke and dust engulfing the front of the patrol. Seconds later the head cam started to bounce violently up and down as Sean began to run, joining his cameraman in a charge towards the blast site.

The IED had knocked down four of the Afghans. They were spread out along the side of the track, flat out in the dust. Amazingly, none of them had died, all of them showing signs of life, groaning together in bewildered unison. Sean and his cameraman set about them with field dressings and morphine, doing what they could to help. One of the Afghans had lost a big chunk of his forearm. Another had a hole like an open mouth in the side of his face.

"We did release this footage," Sean said. "But then it got withdrawn. It's not the best messaging, to be fair."

I suppose it was useful training, watching the entire sequence of an IED blast – by stepping away from the corner of the compound, the point man had saved himself and his colleagues – but it didn't exactly stoke my appetite for my first patrol. If I could just get through it without the IEDs and the misplaced lumps of flesh, I'd be a happy man.

"My tour has been really quiet," Sean said, closing his laptop. "This summer should be much more lively."

"More lively?"

"Definitely." He looked at me thoughtfully. "I envy you."

* * *

I flew to Patrol Base Shahzad with Russ and Ali later that evening, our Merlin skimming the poppy fields of Nad-e Ali under a full moon and a sky thick with stars. I'd never been a huge fan of helicopters, but this was something else. I was actually enjoying myself, the whole flight like something out of a dream. For a second I thought it wouldn't be such a bad way to die, crashing into a field of opium and getting blown to pieces in a massive fireball. At least it would be quick.

After ten minutes of fairground flying we landed with a thud at Shahzad's helipad. The three of us grabbed our kit and stepped out into the moonlight. A gravel pathway led towards the base's old factory, a stone building covered in scorch marks and bullet holes. We headed towards the lights of the main entrance, the Merlin blasting us with sand and grit as it roared back up into the night.

The old factory was home to 3 Para's headquarters. The walls were about two feet thick, giving it the feel of a bunker. It had once housed a construction firm employing thousands of locals from across Nad-e Ali. Before the Taliban got inside and ransacked the place, the firm had built the district's extensive irrigation system, allowing crops and vegetation to flourish. They'd also built and maintained many of the local roads.

We walked into the lobby through a set of thick wooden doors. Five young Paras were sitting at a long table to one side of the room, quietly checking their Facebook messages on a row of laptops. Three other Paras were sitting at a table behind them, watching a football match on the wall-mounted television in the corner. To the other side of the room, hundreds of paperbacks filled a row of shelves cut into the wall. There was also a brew table nearby, with a stack of paper cups and a tea urn.

I noticed that a handful of press cuttings had been stuck to the wall behind the urn. Taking pride of place, right in the middle of the assorted headlines, was a piece by the *Daily Telegraph*'s Thomas Harding. An ex-Para himself, he'd been embedded with 3 Para earlier in the month, producing an article on a Taliban sniper who was targeting soldiers at Patrol Base Qadrat, just a few kilometres up the road:

Two soldiers have been killed and six wounded over the past four months at the base in Qadrat. One Taliban marksman has been killed, but another has eluded efforts to remove him and continues to shoot at soldiers… There have been many near misses with soldiers' armour hit or returning with a hole in their backpacks. Qadrat has been recognized as the most dangerous outpost in Helmand – the site of the highest number of gunshot wounds per soldier.*

---

* *Daily Telegraph* (online), 13th March 2011: 'Paras Play Deadly Game to Draw out Taliban Sniper'.

I read the article carefully, wondering whether we'd be going to Qadrat in the morning. I knew our hosts were planning to take us to one of their outposts, but they still hadn't said which one. The other possibility was Khamaar, a patrol base about which I knew practically nothing. I'd located it on the map, just over two kilometres south-west of Qadrat, but that was the full extent of my knowledge. Whether it also came with its own neighbourhood sniper, I had no idea.

I slept badly that night. We were put up in a transit tent with four other soldiers, all of us dozing fitfully in the darkness. Less than a hundred yards away, a troop of 105-mm guns from 7th Regiment Royal Horse Artillery blasted out fire missions into the early hours of the morning. I lay on a camp cot with my combat jacket for a pillow, staring up at the roof of the tent, a showreel of death and destruction stuck on repeat inside my head, playing out on the black canvas above me. In a matter of hours I'd be going outside the wire for the first time, out on the ground, out in the shit. Surrounded by snipers, IEDs and lumps of rotting flesh…

I got up early. Sunlight started to leak into our tent from 5 a.m. I went outside for a piss and a shave, noting through half-open eyes the perfect crystal blueness of the sky. *If I get hit*, I told myself, *I can look up at that sky and pretend to be somewhere less fucking ghastly.*

I joined Russ and Ali for breakfast. They were sitting at one of the trestle tables inside the dining tent, surrounded by noisy, hungry Paras. Both of them seemed calm and relaxed, the banality of their small talk bringing some much needed perspective to the wild meanderings of my imagination.

"This bacon is terrible," said Ali.

"It's not that bad," said Russ. "I'll eat it."

Things got better after that, lifting my mood considerably. It turned out we were going to Khamaar, which I decided was probably for the best. It hadn't featured in any of the newspaper reports I'd read on Nad-e Ali, so it can't have been that bad. Surely, if it was dangerous, Thomas Harding would've gone there as well?

Our transport arrived shortly after breakfast, three Mastiffs rolling slowly into the vehicle yard through the back gate. Despite their unsophisticated appearance – they looked like giant coffins on wheels – they were still the safest road vehicles we had. Even if we drove directly onto an IED, we'd be OK – unless it was a small nuclear device, we'd just get shaken up.

Although Khamaar was only five kilometres from Shahzad as the crow flies, it took more than an hour to get there. The lumbering Mastiffs were not designed for speed, and the roads in Nad-e Ali were terrible. I sat with Russ and Ali in the back of the rear Mastiff, bouncing around in our seats, trying to get our first look at Afghan life through the narrow bulletproof windows. From what I could tell, it all seemed fairly calm outside, with nothing to suggest a country torn apart by war. Children worked alongside their fathers in the fields, while young men rode along the roads and tracks on their motorbikes. None of them appeared to be carrying any weapons, and none of them looked like they wanted to kill us.

Eventually we got to Khamaar, a base made up almost entirely of tents and Hesco fortifications.* It was much smaller than Shahzad, with no reassuring stone building in the middle of it. Our Mastiff pulled up outside the entrance to the largest tent, next to a smartly painted sign declaring "A Company Headquarters". We opened the heavy doors at the back of the Mastiff and stepped out onto

---

* Containers fashioned out of wire mesh, lined with heavy-duty fabric and filled with rubble and hard core. They are found on ISAF bases throughout Afghanistan.

the gravel, stretching our legs in the sunshine. It was 10 a.m. now, and already feeling hot.

A Company wasted no time getting us out on a patrol. We'd only just dragged our kit from the back of the Mastiff when the company sergeant major – a suitably hard-looking man with cropped hair – stepped out of the headquarters tent and told us we were going straight off.

Within twenty minutes we were standing at the back of a twelve-man patrol, lined up by the loading bay, waiting for the front gates to open. Like everybody else, I was wearing a Mark VII "bullet-stopper" helmet, a full set of Osprey body armour (fitted with chest, back and side ceramic plates), two tiers of pelvic protection – consisting of anti-microbial boxer shorts and a soft Kevlar garment known as a "combat nappy", designed to safeguard your genitals in the event of an IED blast – and a pair of ballistic sunglasses. The only parts of my body that felt exposed were my arms and legs, but even if they got blown off, I knew I'd still have a fighting chance with the surgeons back at Bastion (I knew they'd try to save me, even if I didn't want to be saved).

At least a dozen soldiers from the ANA were also coming, but rather than join us on foot, they were deploying in two Humvees, one at the front of the patrol and one at the back. This would make it harder for Russ and Ali to frame the all-important "partnering" shots, but the Afghans were in no way bothered about that. They were in love with the Humvee, the whole concept of it, gunning the engine and hanging off the doors. Those who couldn't fit inside each vehicle clambered onto the back, crowding around the mounted .50-cal. machine gun. I wasn't about to tell them to dismount, and neither were the Paras.

Having already seen peaceable, non-threatening Afghans going about their business in the fields that morning, I didn't feel too nervous about leaving the base. We turned left outside the gates, walking straight onto a hard-baked dirt road that ran alongside the perimeter wall, keeping a narrow, muddy river on our right. There were a lot of Afghans along the riverbank, most of them young children. They all seemed friendly, many of them smiling and some of them even giving us the thumbs-up.

My job in these circumstances was to stick with Russ, ensuring he didn't wander into the river. His camera's viewfinder left him with no peripheral vision, so whenever he began to stray, I laid a hand on his shoulder, guiding him back into the middle of the road. It wasn't the most demanding task in the world, and I soon found myself starting to relax, all the exaggerated tensions of my sleepless night disappearing. It was actually quite enjoyable, being out on the ground but not feeling in any great danger. The IED threat along the road was low, given its proximity to the base, and the "atmospherics" – the behaviour of the locals against which we measured the likelihood of an attack – were good.

Only one of the youngsters on the riverbank was unimpressed with our patrol: a boy of around seven who pointed a catapult at us. Apparently he had something of a reputation, having slung rocks at soldiers on previous occasions. Our patrol sergeant walked over to him with the interpreter, calmly telling him to put it down.

"If you ever use that catapult on us again," he warned, "I'll tell your father."

The boy lowered his weapon and hurried away.

We set off again, following the river for another hundred yards before arriving at the local bazaar, crowded into the alleyways between two mud compounds. It was a strange, alternative world, the ramshackle stalls offering impossible-to-shift items like slashed tyres and cracked solar panels. In one corner a grimy elder sat in the dirt, welding together two lumps of scrap metal, the sparks flying out in front of us. He didn't spare us a second glance, but the rest of the bazaar's elders stepped out from behind their curious wares and shook our hands. Bearded and craggy-faced, they smiled broadly, showing us their rotten teeth. Unlike the youngsters on the riverbank, they didn't pester us for sweets.

After ten minutes of mostly unintelligible chat, we said our goodbyes to the elders and continued with the patrol, taking our time along a rutted track that eventually led to a remote vehicle checkpoint. It was a poky little compound with a wooden pole for a road barrier, manned by two Afghan policemen. Despite the dangerous nature of their work, searching vehicles for weapons and drugs, they looked deeply bored with their lot in life, their hands thrust into their pockets and their eyes half closed. Our patrol sergeant talked to them for a few minutes, relying heavily on the interpreter, while Russ and Ali captured the moment on film. It was the only chance we were going to get for some partnering shots, our friends in the Humvees having disappeared shortly after we left the base, following their own mysterious route.

We left the policemen to their risky but stultifying work and made our way back to Khamaar. The Humvees rejoined us twenty minutes later, materializing on the dirt road alongside the base. What the ANA had been doing for the last hour was anybody's guess, but they looked happy enough. They took up a position at the back of the patrol and slowly followed us in through the gates.

Back inside the base, alongside the languid Afghan soldiers with their lazy smiles, I must've looked like a grinning, wide-eyed idiot.

Despite the heat and the flies and the dust, I was buzzing. I'd been outside the wire for the first time, met some of the locals, and not died or lost any body parts.

Clearly the Paras had taken us out on a soft patrol, which was fine by me. My aversion to bullets and explosives aside, it suited my team's changing remit. Stories about IEDs and snipers killing our boys served no key-messaging purposes other than to high-light the bravery and commitment of British troops. The Combat Camera Team's role was about more than that: it was evolving into something more progressive. We weren't just here to show the boys having a scrap. We were also here to show the British public that after ten years of fighting, our sacrifices hadn't been in vain: some gains were being made, and Afghanistan was, in some places at least, starting to find its feet.

We stayed in the base's transit tent that night – I slept for a good seven hours this time, spared the bad dreams and the crashing artillery – then after breakfast I interviewed a few of the younger Paras outside the headquarters tent. BBC Four had provided me with a list of questions they wanted asking (examples: *Why is your current operation important? Has it been successful? What is so special about being a Para? Why do you refer to other regiments as "craphats"?*).* Most of them mumbled through their answers, having only submitted to the process at the behest of their com-manders. They may have had no qualms about charging into battle, but they were less keen about fronting up to Russ's camera.

I also tried to interview the patrol sergeant. He'd already said a few words to the camera at the vehicle checkpoint the day before, proving himself to be an intelligent speaker, if a little gruff. In his

---

* If you weren't good enough to wear the Parachute Regiment's maroon beret, you were naturally a craphat.

mid-twenties, he was relatively young for a sergeant, and obviously something of a flyer, destined for great things.

"I don't mean to be awkward," he told me, "but I'd rather not do an interview."

"Why not?"

He grimaced, apparently embarrassed by his excuse. "I'm doing Selection when we get back. I don't want to show my face too much."

By "Selection" he meant "SAS Selection". As excuses went, it was a pretty good one. He was under no formal obligation to give us an interview anyway, and I wasn't about to order him to talk. Even with the younger soldiers I never went beyond some gentle encouragement: if any of them were genuinely opposed to an interview, for whatever reason, I left them alone.

We had more than enough material anyway. Russ started going through all the rushes on his laptop. If time had been an issue, he would've sent the edited footage back to the UK via our portable BGAN satellite dish, using a piece of software known as Livewire.* The BBC Four deadline, however, wasn't for another three weeks, so we could afford to take our time. Once Russ had cut down the footage – and once I'd cleared the resulting edit† – he'd burn it onto a disc and post it back to the UK.

The Mastiffs returned later that afternoon and took us back to Shahzad. They got us in through the gates at 1800 hours, just in time for dinner. After dumping our kit, we joined the queue outside the dining tent, making small talk with the other soldiers as we waited for our scoff.

---

* The size of a laptop, the BGAN allowed us to access the internet via satellite from any-where in the world. Each minute of footage took just over five minutes to send back to the UK through Livewire, at a cost of sixteen US dollars per minute.

† I cleared our material for any operational security issues, as well as any glaring messaging fails.

It was a warm and pleasant evening, the calm only disturbed by the shouting and laughter of kids playing football outside the back gates. Hundreds of feet above the base, the Persistent Ground Surveillance System was watching all, keeping us safe. A blimp with cameras, its coverage of the surrounding area was beamed directly into the old factory's Ops Room, televised on a bank of flatscreens. Any suspect behaviour within a certain radius would be picked up immediately.

"You should've been here in September," said the lieutenant standing next to me. "It was pretty crunchy back then."

Between the hoots and grunts of the young footballers, I could just make out the birdsong in the leafless trees that surrounded the base. "It's amazing," I said. "You've really turned things around."

The lieutenant frowned. He must've been in his early twenties, but the wrinkles that deepened around his eyes took him closer to forty.

"When the summer kicks in, it'll start over," he said. "As soon as the vegetation grows back."

"The vegetation?"

"The leaves on the trees." He glanced up at the blimp. "The cameras will be less effective."

"You think it's going to get bad again?"

He nodded. "I give it another month before it kicks off."

Making Things Look Better

Two days after Nad-e Ali we drove to a small base on the outskirts of Gereshk, home to D Squadron of the Household Cavalry. One of their former troop commanders – Prince William, no less – was getting married in a month. He'd served with D Squadron after passing out from Sandhurst at the end of 2006. To feed the growing demand for wedding-related items in the news, we were going to show the world what his old muckers were getting up to in Afghanistan.

D Squadron shared the base with a company of soldiers from the ANA. The day before our arrival, an insurgent had thrown two grenades at the rickety front gate, injuring three ANA sentries. We drove straight past their replacements on the way in, one of them already with his helmet off, trying to stay a little bit cooler in the midday sun.

The base was like a smaller, grubbier version of Patrol Base Shahzad. It was nice, though, despite the not uncommon grenade attacks. A crumbling stone building housed D Squadron's sleeping area, its half-lit rooms filled with long rows of camp cots. They led through to a bright, airy courtyard that boasted a ping-pong table and two armchairs, giving the base an under-the-radar charm that felt more in keeping with a backpacker community than a military camp.

We stayed on the base that night, then deployed with a troop from the squadron the following morning, going out in a patrol of four Jackals. The open-top wheeled vehicles, which carry up to five soldiers, were great for speed and mobility, but offered little in terms of protection. Russ took a seat in the commander's Jackal, second in the patrol, while Ali and I were given the choice of either the first Jackal or the third.

"But you don't want to go in the front vehicle," said one of the soldiers. "That's the one that always gets blown up."

He was joking, apparently, but then again he wasn't. Ali and I squeezed into the back of the third Jackal.

We rolled out of the front gate, straight into the traffic of Highway 1. The tarmac road was arguably the most important in Afghanistan, covering over 2,000 kilometres, connecting Kabul to Kandahar. Nearly half of the country's population lived within fifty kilometres of it. As we sped through the town of Gereshk, we overtook countless tractors, buses and flatbed trucks. The squadron had been conducting regular patrols along a seventy-kilometre section of the route for the past five months, deterring insurgents from laying IEDs. Security incidents had dropped, and the number of road users was growing steadily.

Two kilometres to the east of Gereshk we turned off Highway 1 and parked up alongside a building site. Dozens of Afghan males ranging from boys to elders were constructing a bazaar, laying the bricks for a series of shops. They'd only just finished the foundations, but it still gave us plenty of decent photo and filming opportunities. We all climbed out of our Jackals and patrolled through the dusty site on foot, following Lieutenant Charlie Talbot, the troop commander. He was a photo and filming opportunity in himself, his fierce eyes, sculpted cheekbones and shock of blond hair giving him the look of a soldierly Billy Idol. With the help of his Afghan interpreter, he talked to the builders as they went about their work in the morning sunshine. Russ followed him closely, recording for posterity their stilted chats about building schedules and security.

After half an hour we left the site and headed out into the greenery of the poppy fields. We patrolled in single file (the "Afghan snake", as we called it), careful to follow in each other's footsteps, even when crossing through the streams. We passed the occasional farmer along the way, tending to his poppy crop, but otherwise it was quiet.

We stayed out in the fields for an hour before returning to the Jackals. As we climbed back into our seats, we heard over the radio the ANA coming under fire about two kilometres to the south-east. They had been destroying a field of poppies – part of a programme known as Government-Led Eradication (GLE) – when they came under attack.

GLE was not something we got involved in. The Afghan President Hamid Karzai had given the initiative his full backing, but it was hugely unpopular with the Afghan people. No compensation was offered to the farmers, many of whom were forced to grow poppy by the Taliban (who had little sympathy for farmers with destroyed crops). ISAF was highly critical of the initiative, but reluctant to intervene. Afghanistan was supposed to be governing itself, and we were supposed to be taking more of a back seat.

Still, Charlie thought it wise to maintain a presence in the vicinity of the contact, just in case it spilt out onto Highway 1. We started up the Jackals and took off east down the road, weaving in and out of traffic for another ten minutes before arriving at an ANA checkpoint. It was a pitiful compound, right on the side of the road, with barely any shade and hundreds of flies. A handful of grim-faced Afghan soldiers watched us closely as we parked in the yard and dismounted. Charlie went inside to speak to the checkpoint commander, while the rest of us took off our boots and wrung out our socks, still wet from the earlier stream crossings. It was 1 p.m. now, and getting uncomfortably hot. I sat on a low wall in the brutal sunlight, watching the steam rise from my empty boots, trying to ignore the growing number of flies buzzing around my pale feet.

Eventually Charlie finished his chat with the ANA commander. He emerged from the commander's "office" – a murky room in a corner of the checkpoint's headquarters – looking unimpressed.

"What a miserable bastard," he said.

He didn't elaborate, but I couldn't help thinking that I'd be pretty miserable too, living in a place like this.

We drove back to base, returning in time for an orders group with the squadron commander, Major Rupert Lewis. He was planning a short operation for the weekend, clearing through a couple of local compounds. All his officers gathered in the briefing room inside the base's headquarters, a small concrete building that faced the squadron's living area. I stood at the back while Russ filmed a few generic shots of Major Lewis and his men.

"We've seen a fair amount of insurgent activity in this area in the last few months," he said, pointing at a highlighted section on the map behind him. "So we can expect it to be a bit spicy."

I made a mental note to add "spicy" to my list of euphemisms for combat. So far on this tour I'd heard "kinetic", "interesting", "crunchy" and "lairy".

Major Lewis continued with the rest of his orders, then asked if there were any questions. One of the junior officers raised his hand.

"What should we do about taking our vehicles through fields and destroying crops?"

It was a sensible enough question. The compounds were in the middle of a series of fields. It was far safer to plough your Jackal through some unfortunate farmer's crop than risk taking the obvious tracks.

"I would rather you drove through a field of wheat," said Major Lewis, "than a field of poppy."

There were puzzled looks all round, so Major Lewis explained his thinking.

"If we destroy wheat, we're allowed to compensate the farmer for lost earnings. But if we destroy poppy – in line with GLE – we're not permitted to give him anything. Which means he'll get it in the neck – quite literally – from the Taliban."

This was the counter-insurgency mindset. Keep the locals happy, if you want to beat the Taliban. It flew in the face of Hamid Karzai's policy on drugs, but apparently we could live with that. It was all part of the ISAF balancing act, trying to keep all the plates spinning at once.

The following day was a Friday, the ANA's day off. The squadron adjusted its routine accordingly, staying on the base to work on vehicle repairs. It gave me a chance to pin down some of the more senior soldiers who'd served alongside Prince William. Army PR in Whitehall had requested interviews with anyone from D Squadron who could reminisce about the royal troop commander.

I managed to locate four NCOs who'd known him. Each took his turn in front of the camera, recalling time spent with the prince in his cavalry heyday.

"He was a good bloke," said his former driver – a lanky, fair-haired corporal. "He made the brews, just like anybody else."

There were no earth-shattering insights, just variations on the theme of "he was one of us". It was fluff, essentially. I even asked each of them to record a wedding-day message.

"Have a great day, hope it all goes well," said the corporal. "You're now well and truly under the thumb."

Russ, Ali and I weren't due to return to Bastion until the following morning, so with the Prince William interviews done, we still had plenty of time to kill. Whenever we were staying in bases like this, we'd sniff around for stories. Ali had already taken pictures of a medic from Port Talbot called Aled, who gave the ANA lessons in first aid. She said he was a good talker, and worth interviewing. Hometown stories about army medics helping the ANA were always an easy sell to local radio stations back in the UK, so I tracked him down.

He looked exhausted when I first saw him, collapsed in one of the armchairs. "I've had one day off in the last six months," he told me in his soft Welsh accent.

"Don't worry, this will only take a moment."

I sat in the chair next to him, holding up my pocket-sized MicroTrack recorder, the little stereo T-mic turned towards his gaunt face.

"What sort of a tour have you had?"

He took a moment to respond. "It's been very busy. We're out on patrol just about every day. Fortunately, I've only had a handful of major trauma cases, which is the way I like it, although I would prefer it if I had none."

"How has the area changed since you came out here?"

"In regards to insurgent activity, it's increased dramatically in the last two months. Certainly since the New Year there's been a huge increase in small-arms fire in our area of operations."

This wasn't what I wanted at all. I steered him towards the bigger picture, hoping for something more positive.

"How many times have you been out here?"

"This is my second tour. I was previously out here in the summer of 2008 with the Royal Irish. That was an extremely busy tour, very demanding, but very rewarding. We had a few tragic days that I would have given anything to change, but it was good, very good."

"And since then, how has the situation improved?"

"The IED threat has increased dramatically," he said. "Back then, it was small-arms fire, RPG fire, indirect fire. Now the IED threat has gone up significantly."

I tried another angle. "What about Gereshk itself? It seems quite normal."

He looked at me for a long moment, thrown by the apparent stupidity of my question.

"Gereshk is a toilet in an oven," he said.

Despite his obvious lack of media training, I did eventually manage to get some positives out of Aled, thanks to an unexpected source.

"What about the Afghan soldiers?" I asked. "What's it like working with them?"

He smiled. "The Afghan soldiers, they still got the crazy fighting spirit that I do love and admire with them. They're still challenging to work with, but they do really enjoy the medical training: they can see the need for it. The counter-IED training, they take it or leave it, but the first aid, they enjoy. So they have progressed somewhat since 2008."

I ended with a few questions about his home town ("What do you miss most about Port Talbot?"), then thanked him for his time. I had about ten minutes of audio, which would take a bit of editing when I got back to the JMOC, but I knew it was good for a couple of clips.

Towards the evening, as it got cooler, many of the soldiers gathered in the seating area outside the squadron's modest cookhouse.

At one of the trestle tables where they normally ate their dinner, a dozen of them had crowded around a laptop. They'd produced a fifteen-minute "tour video", culled from footage off their own hand-held cameras and mobile phones. Peering over their shoulders, I watched a clip of a top-cover man blasting away on his .50 cal., the empty cases falling around his feet to the sound of AC/DC's 'Thunderstruck'.

This particular clip, it turned out, was their only footage of an actual firefight. It was interesting at first, but after about a minute, the unchanging camera angle got a little boring. You couldn't see the enemy anywhere. It could've been filmed on the range. Nothing appeared to be happening, short of someone firing a machine gun at a distant ridge.

One of the soldiers turned to me. "It was much scarier at the time," he said, almost apologetically.

It was often the way with combat footage, regardless of who was filming it. Firefights didn't lend themselves to "holistic viewer experiences". You rarely saw the enemy, and you rarely saw the fall of shot. You just got a succession of images of soldiers firing their weapons at some malevolent presence off-screen. It didn't make for a particularly balanced narrative. What did the enemy look like, exactly? What were they doing? How far away were they? Did they pose a genuine, immediate threat, or were they just dickheads taking potshots?

* * *

We flew back to Bastion the following morning, and got to work on our own masterpieces in the JMOC office. Russ had about eight hours of footage to edit, while Ali had taken hundreds of photographs, from which she would select the best dozen or so. I drafted a quick press release to accompany her pictures, then started listening back through my interview with Aled.

Most of it was unusable. There was no point sending out clips of a British soldier saying that "the IED threat has increased dramatically", for instance. Even if it was true,* what purpose would it have served? I was supposed to be putting out material that helped and supported the cause of our troops. Keeping the British public on side was a part of that cause: it was a part of the war effort. More than ever, the public wanted to know what was being achieved in Afghanistan. After ten years, they didn't want to hear that things were getting worse.

The issue of selective reporting was a moral quagmire, of course, requiring its own coping strategy. Without wanting to get bogged down, I told myself that as long as I was on the military's payroll, I would do the military's bidding. Balance and impartiality – those cornerstones of BBC journalism – were not part of my current remit. When I was no longer in uniform – i.e. when I was back to being a journalist again – then maybe I would rethink my actions. Until then, I would do the job I was being paid to do. I wasn't being asked to kill civilians, and I wasn't being asked to send soldiers to their deaths. I was just a little media bit player, pushing out odds and sods. Joseph Goebbels I was not.

I polished two clips from Aled's interview, both fifteen seconds long, wrote a cue to go with each, then emailed them off to Real Radio Wales, a commercial station based in Cardiff. The first clip

---

* According to Pentagon figures, insurgents planted 14,661 IEDs across Afghanistan in 2010, a 62 per cent increase on 2009, and three times as many as the year before. Improved counter-IED drills and a big rise in the number of Afghan civilians coming forward to report such devices did contribute to improved detection rates, however. The devices killed 430 coalition troops in 2010, slightly down from 447 in 2009 – *Washington Post*, 26th January 2011.

was just human-interest bait, a way of hooking the News Editor. It was Aled's answer to the generic question: "What's the first thing you're going to do when you get home?"

When I get home I'll put the kettle on and go out into the garden. Look over the mountains where I live, smell the air, listen to the sheep and just enjoy the sounds of the countryside. Just peace and quiet and rest.

It was the kind of clip that news editors love. Some could be wary about taking audio from the military, so you had to soften them up.

I put the key messaging into the second clip. News editors would rarely take just one clip when they could have two.

The Afghan soldiers, they still got the crazy fighting spirit that I do love and admire with them. They're still challenging to work with, but they do really enjoy the medical training: they can see the need for it. And I try to make my lessons as interesting as possible for them.

One of the main aims of our job was to highlight the fact that the Afghans would soon be taking over this place (and we would be getting the hell out). From a key-messaging perspective, any media content that failed to include the ANA/ANP was a missed opportunity. Wherever possible, we tried to stress that our presence on the ground was all about "partnering" and "mentoring" the Afghan forces, with a view to the withdrawal of ISAF combat troops by 2015.

Increasingly the Afghan forces were dealing with security incidents on their own, leaving out ISAF altogether. Just that afternoon, as I was editing Aled's interview, the rolling-news channels were full of reports about an attack on a UN compound in Balkh Province. Around two hundred demonstrators had gathered in Mazar-e-Sharif City to protest against the burning of a Koran by a US pastor. The ANP were quickly on the scene, but they did not request ISAF support. Hopelessly outnumbered, they were unable to prevent the demonstrators from storming the compound. Seven UN workers died in the resulting carnage, a number of them beheaded.*

Later that evening, I rang home. I was going to wait until the following day – Mother's Day – but I knew all the headlines about the UN slaughter would've upset my mum. She'd almost certainly assume that Mazar-e-Sharif City – a place I'd never heard of before – was right outside my tent.

"Hello?" she said. Whenever I made my weekly call, it was always Mum who answered.

"Hi Mum, it's me."

"I knew it was going to be you!" She said this every time, her voice always a mixture of happiness and relief. "How are you?"

"I'm fine, absolutely fine." I always tried to make my voice sound as laid-back and untroubled as possible, which was generally quite easy. "How are you?"

"Fine, we're all fine. William is here. We're just having dinner."

I pictured the scene: my brother sitting at the kitchen table underneath the big mirror; my father at the head, his back to the

---

* Terry Jones burned the Koran at his Dove World Outreach Center in Gainesville, Florida on 20th March, before broadcasting the footage on the Internet. His actions triggered a number of protests in Afghanistan. A day after the attack on the UN compound in Mazar-e-Sharif City, there was a violent demonstration in Kandahar City, with around five hundred protesters taking to the streets. Nine Afghan civilians were killed and around eighty wounded.

Welsh dresser; my mother at the other end, nearest the Aga; the dogs invariably sniffing around underneath the table.

"I'll call back in a bit."

"Don't be silly, I'll pass you round. Just say a quick hello."

She handed the phone to my brother first. "How's it going?" he said, as though he'd just bumped into me in the pub. "Everything going OK out there?"

"It's good, all good. How's it with you?"

"Not good," he said. "Bad day for Notts County. Lost two-nil at home to Oldham."

"Never mind," I said. "Keep your chin up."

He passed me over to Dad. He also lamented the Notts County defeat.

"They were terrible," he said. "Absolutely hopeless."

We chatted about Notts County's hopes in the league – a fairly short conversation – then he handed me back to my mother. She lowered her voice.

"That was awful, what happened at that UN place," she said.

"It was. Nowhere near us, though. Other side of the country."

"Good. I'm glad."

I let her get back to her dinner. "I'll call again tomorrow. With it being, you know, Mother's Day."

"I look forward to it."

I went back into the office the following morning. Sunday was normally a fairly relaxed day for the JMOC. There was just the tireless Ali at her desk, poring over her photos.

"Could you clear my images from the Household Cavalry, boss?"

"Sure."

I went through the pictures on her laptop. Our patrol in the poppy fields looked like it had been lifted straight out of a Vietnam movie.

With our MK7 helmets and our multi-terrain-pattern uniform we were dead ringers for American GIs, waiting to be picked off by an unbeatable enemy against a backdrop of lush vegetation and abundant drugs (with no domestic allies in sight). Perhaps if I was truly serving the cause, I would've binned every single image, but I didn't have the heart to wipe out an entire patrol: maybe censorship wasn't my thing after all. In the end I only deleted two images, each showing a soldier in close-up without his ballistic sunglasses (he'd removed them because they'd steamed up, a common problem). Orders from the top, in keeping with our key message that the troops were well equipped.

Op Minimize was announced on the public-address system at midday, just as I was finishing with Ali's photos. Somewhere in theatre, another British soldier's luck had just run out. Whenever one of our guys was killed or badly injured, a temporary ban was enforced on personal calls and social networking until the next of kin had been officially informed.

I logged onto Ops Watch. It wasn't just one of our guys that was hurt: a flurry of reports was coming in from across theatre. Four soldiers from 5 Scots had been caught in an IED blast during a foot patrol in Nahr-e Saraj. The explosive had been placed in a tree. One soldier had shrapnel wounds to his face, two soldiers had wounds to their legs, and another had wounds to his back. Their interpreter took shrapnel to his groin. Also in Nahr-e Saraj, a patrol from the Warthog* group had been hit by an RPG, leaving a soldier with blast wounds to his face, chest and abdomen. Meanwhile in Nad-e Ali a foot patrol from 3 Para had discovered an IED containing roughly 5–10 kg of explosives. As they were clearing the site, they came under fire, leaving one of them with a gunshot wound to the leg.

---

* Tracked vehicles weighing twenty tonnes each, designed for rough terrain.

Op Minimize was lifted the following morning. A number of families back in the UK would've had a very unpleasant Mother's Day, but at least no one had died and, according to the initial reports, no one had lost any limbs.

I tried to ring home. There was always a rush on the phones after Op Minimize, and the system struggled to cope. Unsurprisingly, I'd have to wait until later to get through – everyone on camp was belatedly trying to call their mum.

I went back to work, going through Russ's piece on the Household Cavalry. He'd completed a ninety-second film for the British Army's website ("Armyweb"), which featured an archive of clips you could access via YouTube. The footage showed our drive along Highway 1 and our patrol through the "bazaar in progress", as well as our detour through the poppy fields.

It was a good-looking piece, but there was one shot right at the end that gave me cause for concern. It was a close-up of a poppy flower, with a soldier walking straight past it, as though the purple opium bloom that was ripping this country apart was nothing to do with him.

"That's got to go," I told Russ.

"Sir, that's a really nice shot."

"But he's walking straight past the poppy. Like he's ignoring the problem."

"But we are ignoring the problem."

He moaned a little bit more, but eventually he re-edited the ending, cutting out the offending poppy.

"It ends on a really boring shot now," he said.

Later that evening, news came through that three Afghan police-men had been killed in Herat Province by an "unknown number" of civilians, reportedly angry about poppy eradication. It made me wonder about Russ's film. The shot of the untouched poppy would've gone down perfectly with the farmers out there. They would've loved to see all the uniforms in the land walking straight past their opium crops, ignoring them completely. More than ninety per cent of the world's heroin originated in this country, generating a vast amount of money. What else were the farmers going to grow? Wheat? It was like asking Western bankers to forget about junk bonds and start investing in bread.

War and Peace

The JMOC wasn't the only Media Operations office in Helmand. There was a smaller office at Brigade Headquarters in Lashkar Gah, the province's capital. Known as Task Force Helmand (TFH) Media Operations,* it was run by none other than Colonel Lucas, who'd only recently completed his stint as the commanding officer of the MOG. He spoke to Faulkner on a regular basis, but bosom buddies they were not. Phone conversations between the two of them had a tendency to turn into pissing contests. They never openly fell out – they were too professional for that – but they rarely agreed on anything. Surrounded by the upper echelons of our fighting units, Colonel Lucas had a natural bias towards more offensive operations – anything "kinetic", as far as he was concerned, made for a story. In contrast, Faulkner took a more considered approach, preferring to focus on stories where nothing got blown up.

Our next job was much more in keeping with Faulkner's line of thinking. Three days after our return from Gereshk, we flew out to Forward Operating Base Shawqat to film and photograph a rugby match. A dozen Royal Marines from 45 Commando were playing a team from the ANA on the gravel of their vehicle park. Shawqat had been established within the ruins of a fort built by the British Army in the 1880s during the second Anglo-Afghan war. Some of the original mud walls were still standing, providing a

---

* In our office, whenever we spoke of "TFH", we were generally referring to the Media Operations office, as opposed to TFH as a whole.

nice backdrop to the contest, which was more a jovial chuck-about than an actual match.

We'd been asked to record the event ahead of a charity match between Wasps and Bath taking place at Twickenham on St George's Day later in the month. The organizers were raising money for a number of causes, including Help for Heroes. Our footage would be broadcast on the big screens at half-time, reminding the crowd to spare a thought (and a few quid) for our boys overseas. They would get to see the Royal Marines at play with their ANA colleagues, bonding in a non-threatening environment.

The Royal Marines let them win, of course. The Afghans were hopeless, but then it wasn't exactly their national sport (they struggled in particular with the concept of passing backwards). After the final whistle blew on their unlikely victory (they won by six tries to three), they offered to take on the Marines at cricket, which would no doubt have made for a more evenly fought contest.

It wasn't the most challenging task in the world, filming a game of touch rugby, but I wasn't complaining. The job had its key messages – it's not all shit and misery out here, and we do get on OK with our Afghan colleagues – and we got to stay inside the wire. I wasn't in any great hurry to go wandering around the Green Zone, dodging bullets and side-stepping IEDs. I was quite happy to spend a few days in a non-hazardous environment, staying firmly in one piece.

* * *

After Shawqat we flew to Lashkar Gah, the headquarters of 3 Commando Brigade and the home of Colonel Lucas and TFH. He met us at the helipad, all smiles and promises of spicy, crunchy adventure.

"Welcome to Lashkar Gah," he said.

He took us to the NAAFI* for a cold drink. We sat in a sun shelter next to the base's makeshift volleyball court. He seemed to be in a good mood, although it didn't take him long to launch into a polemic about the Combat Camera Team.

"I want to see you doing more of that." He pointed at the "Combat Camera Team" badge on my left shoulder, poking the word "Combat". "And I'm sure you do too."

"Well, yes, absolutely," I mumbled.

We'd come here to interview Johnny Hall, an ex-army officer from Nottingham who was now working for the Department for International Development (DfID), helping the Afghans to build a highly ambitious business park near the base. *East Midlands Today* had requested the footage, which the JMOC felt would highlight the progress being made in the heart of Helmand's capital. Once again, combat would not be on the menu.

That wasn't to say that Lashkar Gah was a particularly safe place. Just a week earlier, two suicide bombers had tried to blow up the town's courthouse. One of them had detonated his explosive vest prematurely, killing himself and wounding three others outside the main gate, including his partner. The latter had been taken into custody, where he'd told his interrogators there were six other would-be suicide bombers in Lashkar Gah, prepped and ready to go.

This information – reliable or not – had impacted upon our filming schedule. We were going to follow Johnny around a busy market, meeting the locals on foot, but that was now considered too risky. Instead we drove straight to the proposed site of the business park in a convoy of three bulletproof Land Cruisers. Because he was

---

* Navy, Army and Air Force Institutes cafeteria and shop.

working for DfID, Johnny came with his own G4S* security team, composed of burly middle-aged men with designer sunglasses and fancy machine guns. They ploughed through the traffic of Lashkar Gah with ruthless efficiency, cutting up everything in sight, never once allowing the convoy to split.

The business park was apparently going to be built on a patch of wasteland off the main road through Lashkar Gah. We pulled up at the site's entrance, a large archway where Johnny had arranged to meet a small group of local businessmen. They would be overseeing the project, handling the finances and managing the construction. They didn't look much like businessmen when they turned up – they looked more like village elders, bearded and robed – but Johnny seemed happy enough to see them. He greeted each of them personally, smiling and shaking hands, before unfolding a copy of the plans for them all to discuss.

Russ filmed them where they stood, the archway in the background. They were all full of ideas and optimism, pointing out the various imaginary landmarks. I stood off to one side, casting my eyes over the wide empty space, wondering idly whether any of these buildings would ever see the light of day.

I interviewed Johnny after the Afghans had left. He was bright and enthusiastic, brimming with public-schoolboy charm. Pots of government cash aside, I could see why the Afghans liked him.

"I hear them say, 'We don't want the Taliban, we don't want the insurgency here, we want to work with you, what can we do to make that happen?'" he said. "And when you see those changes, you start to have a real sense of optimism."

---

* A British security firm, G4S provided close-protection teams for Foreign Office and DfID staff, allowing them to perform their duties without the obtrusive presence of uniformed soldiers. Ex-regulars with at least seven years' military service and two hostile operational tours under their belts manned most of their teams.

Clearly you had to have some sort of faith in the local population if you were going to get anything done out here, but I found it hard to share in Johnny's optimism. I already knew enough about financial irregularities in this country to know that money had a tendency to disappear into thin air. Rumours of corruption ran through everything. A 2010 UN survey had found that 59 per cent of Afghans viewed public dishonesty as a bigger concern than insecurity and unemployment. During the twelve-month survey period, one Afghan out of two had to pay a kickback to a public official, with the average bribe worth the equivalent of 160 US dollars, totalling almost 38 per cent of the country's per-capita gross domestic product.*

Back at base I wished Johnny the best of luck, and then wandered over to the TFH office to tip my hat to Colonel Lucas. Since our conversation in the sun shelter, I was in no great rush to see him again, but I thought I should do my bit for TFH-JMOC relations before returning to Bastion. At times I felt like an emissary between two rival factions, responsible for maintaining at least a semblance of diplomacy.

He was at his desk when I walked in, chatting to Tom, a huge lumbering commando who for some reason worked in the office as the admin sergeant, booking flights and making tea.

"Christian, come in," he said, turning to me. "Have a seat."

I sat down at a spare desk between the two of them. Tom went back to the spreadsheet on his computer, punching in flight details, while Colonel Lucas gave me his full attention.

"I've got some good news," he said, smiling. "The Afghans have put together their own Combat Camera Team. There are four of them. They're still a little inexperienced, so I think it would be great if you did some training with them."

---

* United Nations Office on Drugs and Crime (online), 19th January 2010: 'Corruption Widespread in Afghanistan, UNODC Survey Says'.

"OK, sir," I said. It sounded straightforward enough. I envisaged some classroom lessons, and maybe a few practical exercises at Bastion.

"I'd like you to go out in the field with them. It would be great if we could get you working together. I'm thinking four week-long operations."

Steering a novice Afghan Combat Camera Team around the Green Zone for a month sounded like madness, but I responded in the way I always did to Colonel Lucas's suggestions:

"OK, sir. Sounds good."

I wasn't about to argue with him. I knew Faulkner would put the kibosh on the whole thing anyway. Even if he liked the idea, he'd never endorse it, simply because it had been dreamt up by Colonel Lucas. I slept soundly that night and returned to Bastion the following morning feeling perfectly relaxed, confident the JMOC would give no ground in this particular pissing contest.

"I agree with Colonel Lucas on this one," said Faulkner when I saw him at breakfast. "I think it's a good idea."

It wasn't a good idea at all. It was a crazy idea. The Green Zone was no place for tutorials on interview techniques and shot sequencing. The tactical implications of seven of us in a huddle, faffing about with microphones and cameras in the middle of a firefight, didn't bear thinking about.

"It might be a little ambitious, sir," I said. "If I'm being honest."

Faulkner thought about this for a long moment, chewing his bacon slowly.

"Four week-long operations is a big commitment," he said finally. "Maybe go for a more gradual approach."

"OK, sir. We'll start with some classroom training."

* * *

Grateful that sanity and the natural order had been restored, I went over to the RSOI training area with Russ later that afternoon to film a first-aid presentation. The recording was to be sent back to the UK, where it would be shown to troops as part of their pre-deployment training. Around forty new arrivals sat in a tent while a combat medic called Sergeant Melvin ran through the various ways of treating casualties out on the ground.

Russ and I had already seen the presentation during our first week in theatre, but it was still powerful. Sergeant Melvin – a surprisingly cheerful individual, given his job – started by emptying a one-litre bottle of blackcurrant squash onto the ground, representing the large puddle of blood that would immediately result from a trau-matic amputation.

"Is that a lot of blood?" he asked. "Who thinks that's a lot of blood?"

There were a few mumbled "yeahs" from the audience.

"It's not a lot of blood, guys. It's only twenty per cent of your blood volume. Guys out on the ground can lose up to three limbs, four limbs, and they're still surviving."

He pointed to a nearby pile of tourniquets, compression band-ages, chest seals and haemostatic dressings.

"It's because of all that kit over there that you get issued, and it's because you guys are doing a fantastic job on the ground, sorting your mates out."

The aim of the presentation, more than anything, was to instil confidence in the new arrivals, and to reassure them. As well as demonstrating the various applications of the issued kit – all revi-sion – Sergeant Melvin also reeled off some comforting statistics about injuries.

"In February last year, there were 266 battle casualties across the operational spectrum, and eleven per cent of that number were British casualties – and that's not many. And again, this year in February, we only had eleven casualties. This month so far, we've only had seven battle casualties out of 9,500 people. That is not a lot, guys. If you work that out as a percentage, your chance of getting injured is very, very slim at the moment."

As well as going out on regular patrols in the Green Zone, Sergeant Melvin could also draw on his experiences at the hospital in Bastion, working shifts in the Emergency Department.

"There's been some positive feedback from the hospital," he said. "The insurgents are struggling to get hold of high-grade explosive. They're using home-made fertilizer, which is resulting in more lower-limb amputations and fragmentation injuries. It's not the high amputations that we used to get, it's lower-limb. And that's a lot easier to deal with. I was in the hospital the other day, and we treated an Afghan farmer who'd been digging in his field when he hit a device. What injuries do you think he suffered? What do you reckon? Lower limbs and all that kind of stuff? Do you want me to tell you what he came in with? Fragmentation injuries. Because the quality of the device was that bad, he just got fragged. So that's real positive stuff, guys. You need to take that away."

Later that afternoon, an incident occurred in Nahr-e Saraj that seemed to confirm Sergeant Melvin's comments. A soldier from 5 Scots was caught up in a blast during a patrol near Patrol Base 3. Rather than losing both his legs, he'd just lost his left foot. The IED – containing around five kilograms of home-made explosive – had only partially detonated.

It got me thinking again about our prospects with the Afghan Combat Camera Team. Maybe deploying into the Green Zone with them wouldn't be such a bad idea after all. Maybe things were getting better, and we'd be just fine.

Two-Headed Beasts

On the afternoon of Friday 15th April a man in ANP uniform walked into the police-headquarters complex in Kandahar. He waited in the courtyard outside the office of the Chief of Police, Khan Mohammed Mujahid. A former Mujahidin leader, Mujahid had already survived two previous attempts on his life. As he emerged from his office to get into his car, the man in ANP uniform stepped forward and detonated the explosives packed into his suicide vest. Mujahid died in the blast, along with two other ANP officers. Three others were wounded. The Taliban claimed the dead bomber as one of their own.

I read about the attack while sitting in the JMOC, wondering how long it would be before something loud and unpleasant happened at Bastion. When it came to insider attacks, there was no real fighting season in Afghanistan. They happened all over the country on a depressingly regular basis.

The following morning, a man in ANA uniform walked into a meeting between US troops and soldiers from the 201st ANA Corps at Forward Operating Base Gamberi in Laghman Province. There were around forty people in the room. The man in ANA uniform threw a number of hand grenades at them, before detonating several more on his vest. A few of the soldiers had a split second to hit the floor, and a few managed to jump out of the windows. But only a few. Five US soldiers and four ANA soldiers died in the attack, with seventeen others injured. A US civilian and an Afghan inter-preter were also killed.

"The Afghan and foreign forces had a meeting as usual, and an explosion took place," said Major Mohammed Osman, a spokes-man for the 201st Corps. "We found one leg that we expect might be from the suicide bomber."

The Taliban claimed responsibility for the attack. Their spokes-man Zabiullah Mujahid said: "We had recruited this man one month ago, and he was serving as an Afghan soldier for the last month."* He added: "Using these kinds of attacks is very useful for us in recruiting someone and working inside Afghan forces. This inflicts more casualties and does not cause any civilian casualties. We have many more youths who are already in Afghan military ranks waiting for their chance to attack."

Security was now being tightened at Bastion. All ISAF personnel entering Shorabak, the large ANA training base located within the camp's boundaries, were ordered to carry loaded weapons. The ANA was expanding at a rapid rate – they were aiming for 195,000 troops by 2013 – inevitably growing the "threat from within".

Some of the more circumspect among us – myself included – also took to carrying a weapon in our own section of camp. The canteen, for a start, was the most obvious place for an attack, with thousands of us sitting down for breakfast, lunch and dinner at the same time every day. Russ and Ali thought I looked ridiculous fetching my Weetabix and fruit salad with a Browning 9-mm pistol on my hip, but that didn't bother me. There was a thin line between being prepared and being paranoid, and I was more than happy to cross it.

---

* *New York Times* (online), 16th April 2011: 'Blast Kills 9 at Afghan Base, Including 5 from NATO'.

Two days after the killings in Laghman Province, a man in ANA uniform walked into the Defence Ministry in Kabul, hours before a visit from the French Defence Minister. He got up to the second floor before opening fire on ANA soldiers, killing two and injuring seven others. A security guard shot him dead before he could detonate his explosive vest. The unstinting Zabiullah Mujahid claimed the attacker was a Taliban sleeper agent who'd been serving in the ANA for three years and working in the Defence Ministry for six months, while the ANA's military spokesman, General Zahir Azimi, insisted the investigation was still ongoing.

"We don't know whether he was a member of the army or not," said General Azimi. "All I can say is that he was wearing an Afghan National Army uniform. It doesn't mean he was an army soldier. You know, finding a uniform is easy. They can find it anywhere, and they can make it. People sell military equipment in the bazaar. We have collected and confiscated uniforms several times, but it's hard to collect all of them." He added: "We have set up a security team who is watching suspicious people inside military forces, but it's hard to recognize them."*

*   *   *

Two days later, on 20th April, we flew to Kabul to cover the most banal of stories. A team of civilian repairmen were visiting all the ISAF camps in the Afghan capital, carrying out maintenance checks on gym equipment. We were going to follow their progress.

---

* *New York Times* (online), 18th April 2011: 'Suicide Bomber Attacks Afghan Defense Ministry'.

Faulkner felt it made for a worthwhile story. Apparently it would highlight the fantastic training facilities available to both British and Afghan troops. He dismissed a request from TFH for the Combat Camera Team to deploy instead on a recce with 24 Commando Engineer Regiment, who were preparing to build a bridge over the Nahr-e Bughra Canal in Nahr-e Saraj.

"Media operations should be one big happy family," Faulkner said, following another terse phone conversation with Colonel Lucas. "Not this two-headed beast."

The flight to Kabul took just over an hour. There were about forty troops in our Hercules, half of them soldiers from the ANA. They all sat together down one side of the aircraft, while the British and Americans sat down the other side. The lights were dimmed for most of the flight, making reading difficult, and the noise drowned out any attempts at conversation. Most of us just slept for the journey, our spongy little earplugs reducing the roar of the engines to a hypnotic drone.

Kabul was much cooler than Bastion – I felt the difference at the airport, as soon as I stepped off the back of the Hercules. At the higher altitude, daytime temperatures sank by around ten degrees. Being tucked into the side of the Hindu Kush, the landscape was also very different: unlike the desert that encircled Bastion, Kabul was surrounded by mountains.

I walked over to the terminal with Russ and Ali. All the flight baggage had been dumped on the tarmac outside a set of double doors beneath a sign that read: "Welcome to Kabul". We picked up our kit and walked through to the terminal concourse, a bizarre hybrid of defence installation and retail hotspot. It bristled with shops and cafés, giving it the air of a militarized tourist zone. Soldiers and airmen in a mixture of uniforms – German, Polish,

Estonian – drank coffee and browsed through all the strange items on sale. If you were in the market for ISAF crockery or a War on Terror chess set (the white pieces featuring the likes of Barack Obama and Donald Rumsfeld, the black pieces led by Osama bin Laden), it was a good place to waste some money.

The city had suffered a rash of suicide bombings in recent weeks, ramping up the threat level. Our transport from the airport consisted of two Ridgebacks – chunky, heavily protected vehicles, not dissimilar to Huskies. The drivers took us to a nearby British base called Camp Souter, stopping at four checkpoints along the way. It was only 800 metres from the airport, but the journey took more than twenty minutes. We sat in the back of the second Ridgeback with a signaller returning from R&R. He was based at Souter, and had never deployed anywhere else.

"It's like a concrete city," he moaned. "I'm sick of it."

He made concrete sound like a bad thing, but to me it meant security, electricity and decent showers. Outside the base's accommodation block we were met by the admin sergeant, who led me to my own individual room: it had proper walls, a high ceiling with a fan and a television set. Next to the single bed was a tall window with a view across the rooftops of Kabul. It was dark now, and the lights of the city stretched out all the way to the foot of the mountains.

I met up with Russ and Ali a short time later in the base's coffee shop. They were sitting at the bar, chatting to a colour sergeant who looked like a leathery, middle-aged version of Robbie Williams. He was based down the road at Camp Julian, training ANA officers.

"It's not the ANA doing it," he said. "It's Taliban that have infiltrated."

He was referring to the recent surge in green-on-blue attacks. To my mind, he was stating the bleeding obvious, but I wasn't about to say that to his face.* I knew there were Special Forces based at Julian – we'd been told we couldn't film there for that very reason – and I knew that some of them were involved in ANA training. With no insignia on his uniform, it was clear he wasn't your average soldier.

"The ANA commander on our base can usually spot any dodgy recruits," he said, "but it's getting harder. More and more recruits are coming through. I've got a bunch of ex-Mujahidin starting on Saturday."

"They must be getting on a bit," I said.

"Most of them are over fifty, but they're pretty good," he said. "And they're less likely to explode."

Suicide bombers tended to be young men, if not children. Grizzled war veterans over the age of fifty might snap and grab a machine gun and kill everybody in the room, but they were less inclined to go down the more painstaking route of martyrdom. The ex-Mujahidin were old-school warriors: if they had a grievance with you, they would fight you, but generally try to stay alive at the same time.

As it happened, Mujahidin Victory Day was due to be marked the following week. It commemorated the Mujahidin's overthrow of the communist government in 1992, three years after the withdrawal of Soviet troops. As a public holiday, occasioning various parades and civic events, it was naturally a focal point for the insurgents,

---

* In fact, his statement was neither obvious nor correct. A NATO review of green-on-blue attacks published two months after this conversation presented a more varied set of findings. It analysed all such attacks from 2005 to the present day – there were forty-four incidents, resulting in fifty-two coalition deaths – and found that 38 per cent of them were the result of "emotional, intellectual or physical stress due to presence in a combat environment". In addition to combat stress, the investigation concluded that 19 per cent of "insider attacks" were caused by insurgents encouraging or blackmailing Afghan soldiers and police to attack coalition forces. Posing in bought or stolen uniform accounted for just under 10 per cent of the attacks, while the remaining 35 per cent of incidents were "unexplained". Source: the ANSF Vetting Process (8th February 2011) and 'Combating the Insider Threat' (16th July 2011) by Professor Derek Reveron, US Naval War College.

who always tried to mark the day with some sort of atrocity. A number of possible attacks had already been identified, and the threat level had risen accordingly.

We were told as much the following morning, during the brief for our journey to Camp Alamo. One of the civilian repairmen was going there to fix some running machines in the gym. It was still a lame story, nothing had changed, and I had no idea where it was going. I wasn't miserable, though. The sun was shining, and the temperature was a balmy 22°C. Breakfast had been fantastic – I'd poured a ridiculous amount of golden syrup on my pancakes and wallowed in the sugary taste of Western civilization. Life was good.

Russ and Ali squeezed into the back of a Toyota Land Cruiser with the repairman, who was understandably bemused as to why his assignment merited the attention of a Combat Camera Team. I sat up front with the driver and we all set off for Alamo, hitting the chaotic streets of Kabul in bulletproof comfort.

The traffic in the city centre may have been a lawless free-for-all, but it was nothing compared to the mayhem outside Alamo. The scene at the front gate was like something out of *Wacky Races*, with all manner of jeeps, trucks and lorries jockeying for position, everyone trying to get in and out of the base at the same time. The front gate itself, right on the Jalalabad Road, consisted of a pathetic wooden barrier, held up by a rather worried-looking Afghan soldier. Nobody wanted to sit in traffic outside any military base in Afghanistan, but this road in particular was notorious. All of the ISAF bases along a five-mile stretch out of the city centre bore the brunt of a gruelling Taliban schedule, the insurgents targeting the front gates with varying degrees of success. Camp Phoenix, a little farther down the road, had been on the receiving end of the latest attack just two weeks earlier. Their hefty fortifications put Alamo to shame, and the sentries, American soldiers from 1st Squadron 134th Cavalry Regiment, had been able to stand their ground. Two suicide bombers had charged the front gate and blown themselves up, while insurgents on the road had peppered the sentry posts with machine-gun fire and rocket-propelled grenades. Two Americans were injured, but not seriously. Some damage was caused to the gate, but it was soon repaired.

With no suicidal insurgents to greet us, we managed to get through the gate at Alamo unharmed. It was a joint base, shared between the Afghans and the US, with the ANA occupying the outer section. We drove past hundreds of ANA soldiers on our way in: some marching down the main drag, others leaning over the concrete balconies of their three-storey barrack blocks, elbows resting on damp laundry, and others just sitting on the grass verges in the sunshine.

The American section of Alamo was like a base within a base. Their entrance was a good deal more secure, with Hesco fortifications and a number of unsmiling guards. We parked outside and walked through a steel turnstile into a gravelled area that led to a series of two-storey concrete offices, behind which sat the gymnasium. It was a wooden, single-storey building which the Americans shared with a small contingent of British troops. We followed the repairman inside, into a room filled with weightlifting equipment. Two men in tight, sweat-soaked T-shirts were working on their bulging arms, but the rest of the kit was unused.

"I hope it gets busier," said Ali.

"The cardiovascular machines are right through here," said the repairman.

We followed him into a smaller adjoining room. It was crowded with running machines, but not much else. A tubby middle-aged woman in a hijab and a pink tracksuit was walking at the slowest speed possible on one of them. She looked like she was about to keel over.

"I need to sort out the belt on this one," said the repairman. He started to dismantle one of the machines.

"Do you want me to film this, boss?" said Russ.

"You might as well," I said. "Try to get the Afghan woman in the background."

"She's not Afghan, boss."

"How do you know?"

"She's got a Jordanian flag on her tracksuit."

I looked closer at the exhausted woman. She did indeed have a small Jordanian flag on her chest.

"This is ridiculous," said Ali. "I can't believe we're even doing this."

"Well, we're here now. Let's just shoot what we can."

We loitered in the cardiovascular section for a few more minutes, getting some token shots and footage, then moved back into the weights room.

"Go fairly tight on those guys," I said to Russ, nodding towards the two iron-pumpers. "We don't want this place to look half empty."

"They're not Brits," he said. "They're Americans. I heard them talking."

"Film them anyway."

The whole thing was farcical, but you had to give the lemon a bit of a squeeze before you threw it away. Faulkner hadn't promised the material to any media outlets: he'd only made a vague reference to some fitness magazines. There were always other stories to find – we'd just have to sniff around. I'd already arranged to film with the Afghan Air Force in two days' time, so our trip wasn't going to be entirely wasted.

Back at Souter, we did find something else to cover. All the British troops on the base, members of the Joint Support Unit, were holding an Easter service. About seventy of them had formed up on the main concourse running through the middle of the base, while the padre gave a reading and led them through a number of hymns.

Ali took the pictures and I wrote up the press release. She emailed all the material to a number of news agencies back in London, in the hope that some of the shots would make the papers the following day. It was a nice little Easter story, reminding the folks back home that the boys were still out here, bringing a sense of order and decency to this chaotic country (there were no Afghans in any of the shots – which was hardly surprising – but you couldn't have everything). The British papers were always looking for material to fill out their pages over the bank holiday, so it had a good chance of getting picked up.

One of the British papers – the *Daily Star* – did indeed pick up one of Ali's pictures. Unfortunately, it ran the image alongside a story about an April Fool's gag in *Soldier* magazine that had backfired:

Hundreds of troops fell for a hoax to convince them "sexist" ranks such as "guardsman" were to be ditched. Angry soldiers flooded Internet forums when their official magazine said they would be given new gender-neutral titles. The article claimed a guardsman would be called a "protector", "sentinel" or "escort" and craftsmen would be known as "artificers" or "tradespersons". It blamed EU equality laws. But the April Fool worked too well and many squaddies fell for it, complaining on blogs and message boards.*

---

* *Daily Star* (online), 25th April 2011.

I knew nothing about this story – it was fluff, really – but it was parked right alongside Ali's picture of the soldiers at Souter, singing on Easter Sunday. There was a separate caption beneath the image to that effect, but the whole thing fell under the main headline "Armed Farces".

Ali was disappointed, understandably, but there wasn't a lot we could do about it. Once our material was distributed, dropped into the laps of tabloid editors and TV producers, it was out of our hands. We just had to hope that they would use it responsibly, and within its original context. If they decided to go "off message" and come up with a banner headline like that, then we were powerless to stop them. There were no issues relating to operational security, so no one was going to die. It was just a messaging failure. We could moan about it for a while, but then we'd just have to accept it and get on with the next job.

* * *

On the Easter Monday we returned to the airport to film the Afghan helicopter pilots. They were members of the Air Interdiction Unit, supporting the ANP on counter-narcotics operations. More than thirty of the pilots and air crew had previously undergone training with the RAF at Boscombe Down. This gave us an angle for the British media, but we were also planning to push the story towards the Afghan media itself, targeting outlets like Kabul's Tolo TV.

The Air Interdiction Unit was based in a series of newly built offices and hangars to the north of the airport's main terminal. Known as North KAIA, it was home to the headquarters of the rapidly expanding Afghan Air Force, which at the time consisted of forty-four helicopters (mostly Russian-made Mi-17s) and thirteen fixed-wing aircraft (mostly C-27A Spartan transports, replacing their old Antonovs) in serviceable condition. The compound was officially opened in May 2009, following a construction process that cost seventy-seven million dollars, making it the single largest wartime construction project in NATO's history. Thirteen million dollars alone were spent on security upgrades aimed at thwarting bomb attacks on the gates. The opening saw more than two hundred ISAF personnel move into the compound, where they enjoyed a relatively high standard of living, working alongside their Afghan colleagues.

We met a group of US and Afghan pilots on the nearby flight line. They took us out in their Mi-17s to a range in the mountains, giving the door gunners a chance to blast away at some targets. The prospect of a two-hour flight on a creaky old Russian helicopter didn't exactly fill me with joy, but at least there was plenty of room inside. I stretched out my legs near the back of our shuddering airframe while Russ and Ali hovered around the cockpit and the two door gunners. The Stakhanovite groan of the engines meant interviews were out of the question, so I put on my ear defenders and tried to make myself as comfortable as possible.

Back on the ground I interviewed one of the Afghan pilots. He'd trained at Boscombe Down, and said he liked England and missed the fish and chips. Like a lot of the Afghan pilots, his English was good, and we didn't need an interpreter. Many of them had completed an intensive language course at the compound's so-called "Thunder Lab", a highly regarded English immersion programme that prepared Afghan officers for pilot training. That was a story in itself, and I'd already made arrangements to come back and film there when the next course started.

We made the short trip back to Souter in the evening. The plan was to edit the material the following day, then fly back to Bastion on Wednesday. We were keen to get out of Kabul before Mujahidin Victory Day on Thursday. The raised threat levels meant a risk of flights being cancelled, and we didn't want to get stuck.

On Wednesday morning I was killing time with Ali on the main terrace at Souter, chatting and drinking coffee in the sunshine, when the sirens at the airport went off. Our flight wasn't due to leave until the evening, but it didn't sound good. I went over to the Ops Room to find out more. The sirens were loud and continuous, rising and falling like something out of a Second World War air raid.

The reports from the airport were sketchy at first, and it took a few hours for a detailed picture to emerge. An Afghan pilot had walked into a meeting at North KAIA carrying two firearms, following an argument moments earlier. He'd shot dead eight US servicemen, most of them air-force officers, and a US contractor. Five Afghan troops were also injured. According to later reports, the gunman also suffered a serious injury himself. He left the room and was later found dead in a different part of the building.

"After the shooting started, we saw a number of Afghan army officers and soldiers running out of the building," said Colonel Bahader, a spokesman for the Afghan Air Force. He told reporters that one Afghan was shot – in the wrist – but the rest had suffered broken bones and cuts. "Some were even throwing themselves out of the windows to get away."

In the days that followed, the identity of the gunman was revealed as Ahmad Gul, a forty-eight-year-old pilot with decades of military experience, having been trained during the Soviet Union's occupation. His brother, Mohammed Hassan Sahibi, gave an interview to Tolo TV, claiming that Gul had been struggling with financial problems.

"He served his country for years," he said. "He loved his people and his country. He had no link with Taliban or al-Qaeda. He was under economic pressures and recently sold his house. He was going through a very difficult period of time in his life."*

At the same time, the Taliban released a statement claiming responsibility for the attack. Spokesman Zabiullah Mujahid said the gunman had impersonated an officer, gaining access to the compound with the help of others.

"One suicide attacker managed to attack an Afghan military unit and has managed to kill many Afghan and international soldiers," he said. "We had worked hard on this plan for a long time. He was co-operating with us since long time and he was providing us information about military operations for a long time."†

Unsurprisingly, our flight back to Bastion on the Wednesday evening was cancelled. The following day – Mujahidin Victory Day – the threat level was through the roof. The morning flight was dropped, then an afternoon flight was hastily organized, taking off after lunch. We had no trouble getting three seats on it, given the reluctance of most people to fly in such circumstances. According to the latest intelligence reports, six suicide bombers were on standby in the city, apparently in the vicinity of the airport.

After we'd checked in, we waited in the sunshine outside a busy Greek café. From our table we could see directly onto the main runway, where planes were once again landing and taking off. As we chatted about the events of the last few days, drinking our coffee, a US Air Force officer came over and introduced himself. He'd seen the Combat Camera Team badge on my arm and, working as a press officer himself, he wanted to meet me.

"They just put all the caskets on the plane," he said. "It's a real shame."

---

* CBS News (online), 27th April 2011: '9 Americans Dead after Afghan Officer Opens Fire'.
† CNN World (online), 28th April: 'Man Opens Fire on Americans in Kabul; 9 Dead'.

"It's terrible." I assumed he was talking about his nine dead countrymen – which he was, but only indirectly.

"Yeah, you just missed it," he said. "Real shame. You could've got some nice shots."

He went back to his own table, while I marvelled at the capacity of the military machine to just roll onwards. The bodies would be flown home – after a few formalities, the families would be left to suffer their loss for the remainder of their days – and the rest of us would just continue with the mission, our questionable instincts telling us that death was something that only ever happened to other people.

About twenty minutes after my bizarre exchange with the USAF officer, a young RAF officer called Jack Humphrey introduced himself to me. We'd spoken over the phone a week earlier about a possible story on the "Thunder Lab". He looked pale and drawn, like he was about to faint. He worked in the set of offices where the shooting had taken place.

"We've all been moved over to this side of the airport," he said. "All my personal kit is still in one of the buildings that have been locked down."

He looked badly shaken up. The Afghan pilot was a well-known figure who had just "flipped" and started shooting. All the Americans had been armed, but they hadn't stood a chance.

"In the lobby of the building where it happened, there's a picture of him on the wall," he said. "He's shaking hands with one of the guys he killed."

We eventually got our flight back to Bastion. It was only half full, but still there was the usual clustering of ISAF troops and Afghans. This time it was a group of interpreters, about a dozen of them, eyeing us warily from their side of the plane. For once, I didn't fall asleep. I stayed awake in the half-light, wondering what they really thought about us, wondering what hope there was for "partnering", and wondering what hope there was for this country.

Shorabak

The day after our return from Kabul, we went to Shorabak to cover a party being thrown to celebrate the Royal Wedding. In the weeks leading up to this historic event, the BBC had put in numerous requests for a live link-up with the Household Cavalry. Specifically, they wanted a hundred soldiers from D Squadron to gather in a tent at Bastion and watch the ceremony on a giant screen, while a camera beamed their reactions back to the UK. Given D Squadron's operational commitments, it was a wildly unrealistic demand, but rather than organize a more practical alternative for the BBC, the JMOC simply told them that it couldn't be done.

"We're trying to fight a war here," said Harriet repeatedly. Four months into her tour, she still hadn't left the base, but this was one of her favourite phrases.

In the end, the good old Mercians threw a party instead, albeit without the live link-up. They'd recently moved into Camp Tombstone, a base within a base at Shorabak. Having taken over the role of Brigade Advisory Group from the Irish Guards, they had particularly close connections with the ANA, so a load of Afghans were also invited. It was a perfect piece of PR: British soldiers out in Afghanistan enjoying a barbecue with their Afghan counterparts, celebrating the Royal Wedding. They'd filled a large open-ended tent with benches, trestle tables and two widescreen televisions, so everyone could sit down together and watch the ceremony. The atmosphere was friendly and relaxed – some of the Mercians were even wearing Hawaiian shirts – although everyone was still carrying their pistols, just in case one of the Afghans took a dislike to the steak and went berserk.

After I'd finished my steak – which was actually quite nice – a rather gaunt Danish major sat down next to me. He made me feel hungry again, just looking at him.

"My name is Mikkel Hedegaard," he said. "I am in charge of the Afghan Combat Camera Team."

"I'm sorry?"

It turned out he was a media-liaison officer for the ANA. He was based at Tombstone, and the Afghan Combat Camera Team fell under his jurisdiction. He'd already spoken to Colonel Lucas, and was keen to get us all out in the field together.

"There is a big operation coming up," he said. "At the end of next month. Operation Omid Haft."

"I know about Omid Haft."

"The Afghan team is very enthusiastic, but they're inexperienced. They need you out there with them."

"We'll be happy to help," I said, choosing my words carefully. "As long as we get enough time to train them properly."

"Yes, we could do some training here. I think a week would be good."

It sounded reasonable enough. At least he understood the need for a "gradual approach".

"But we should not overdo the training," he added. "I think four hours a day is about right. They won't do any more than that."

Mikkel suggested a daily timetable from 9 a.m. till 11 a.m., taking three hours off for lunch, then resuming in the afternoon from 2 p.m. till 4 p.m. As a work schedule, it was probably a bit too gradual, but Mikkel insisted it was as much as we could hope for.

"That is just how it is," he said. "It is the Afghan way."

* * *

We returned to Shorabak the following morning, this time to cover the official opening of its Regional Military Training Centre. Our content from the wedding celebration had gone down quite well – BBC West Midlands, home patch of the Mercians, had taken the footage, while the *Sunday Express* had picked up the stills – but I had my doubts about the market for a story on raw Afghan recruits. There wasn't an abundance of angles for the British media – even the instructors were Afghans – so there was a chance our messaging would just disappear. If there were any British mentors on the scene, then we'd be able to cook something up – otherwise, the story would probably go nowhere.

We went to the opening with Dougie, a flight lieutenant from the RAF reserves who'd only just arrived in theatre. He'd moved into the empty bed space next to mine, his arrival having been delayed by six weeks after he broke his ankle skiing. Dry-humoured, with a large, friendly face, he was an easy man to like, and I was already enjoying working alongside him. I wasn't sure what his job at the JMOC actually involved – he was in charge of Strategic Messaging, a new role in the office which was so all-encompassing it could've meant anything – but he seemed to know what he was doing. He drove us to Shorabak in the JMOC minibus, telling us about the heightened alert state on the way.

"They think a suicide attack is imminent," he said. "Apparently the Taliban are planning a spectacular on Bastion in the next few days."

When we pulled up outside the gates at Shorabak, the US sentries confirmed what Dougie had told us. The opening was still going ahead, but any ISAF troops who weren't directly involved with the ceremony would be risking their lives unnecessarily.

We drove in anyway. We were the Combat Camera Team, what else were we going to do?

"You can't drop everything every time the threat level goes up," said Dougie, who also felt a professional obligation to ignore the warning. "We'd never get anything done."

More than eight hundred ANA recruits had formed up on the parade square in the middle of the base, many of them with their issued M16 rifles. They'd just started their eight-week basic training course, after which they'd join the various ANA *kandaks* (battalions) across Helmand. The sheer volume of recruits who would be passing through the training centre was staggering. The next intake was set to almost double in size, with more than 1,500 recruits expected.

We could see a lot of American soldiers around the edge of the parade square, all of them carrying weapons, all of them looking jumpy. British soldiers, meanwhile, were in short supply, and the few who were to be seen were all climbing into their various vehicles and driving away.

"It doesn't look too good," said Dougie. "Hang on."

He pulled the minibus over to one side and jumped out, asked a few questions of the twitchy Americans, then came back thirty seconds later.

"There's really no point you being here, guys," he said. "I'm going to take a few pictures, but I don't think there's more to it than that. The Brits have all disappeared."

Dougie had only been in theatre for a matter of days, but he seemed anxious to stay out of the JMOC. I knew his work kept him tied to his desk for a lot of the time, but I didn't think the cabin fever would kick in this quickly. He'd brought his own camera along with him, and he was already desperate to prove he had a role outside the confines of the office.

"Are you sure you're going to be OK?" I asked. "I don't want to abandon you."

"Don't worry, I'll be fine," he said. "I'll get a lift back with one of the Americans."

We left him there, clutching his camera, surrounded by hundreds of Afghans and a smattering of nervous Americans. He seemed happy enough.

Russ, Ali and I spent the rest of the morning back at the JMOC, drinking coffee, editing some of our material from Kabul, and generally taking it easy. I didn't like sitting in the office for hours at a time – there wasn't much bonhomie, Faulkner tending to discourage small talk – but in keeping with my general desire to stay alive, I could see its attractions.

Dougie returned to the JMOC just before lunchtime, having successfully hitched a ride in a Humvee. He walked back into the office with a huge grin on his face.

"It all got really jumpy," he said. "All the Americans had rounds up the spout. Everyone was worried about a green-on-blue."

"Did you get some good shots?" asked Ali.

"I did eventually, but just after you left, this huge crowd of Afghans came charging towards the parade square. All the Americans thought it was some sort of coordinated attack, and were reaching for their weapons."

"What happened?"

Dougie laughed. "They were all chasing a sheep. It had escaped from the kitchens. It was their dinner."

He sat down and went through his pictures. He'd clearly enjoyed the whole experience, but within a few hours he looked bored and tired again, stuck behind his desk. He wanted something else to happen, something new to lift him, but his other work commitments wouldn't allow it. Phone calls had to be made, and emails had to be sent. It was the office experience, transferred into Bastion, and it didn't appear to suit him one little bit. He'd volunteered for this tour hoping for some sort of profound experience, and all he was getting – with the exception of the sheep incident – was the boredom of everyday life.

Dougie had another five months to look forward to, sitting behind that desk. It wasn't going to get any more exciting for him, not any time soon. He was going to have to start "managing his expectations", as Faulkner liked to say. Otherwise things were going to get much worse – not "bad day in Helmand" worse, of course: just "pointless, meaningless, what the hell am I doing here" worse.

OBL Dead

On the morning of Monday 2nd May, we took a Merlin to Lashkar Gah for a short tasking at the nearby ANP training centre. The pilot threw it around like a lunatic, as though he was bored shitless with the whole Afghan experience. Coming into town, he took us incredibly low over the rooftops, then soared upwards and almost barrel-rolled, before dropping us straight down into the base, throwing up a huge cloud of dust. Ordinarily I would've hated it, but since getting to Afghanistan I'd learnt to love flying in helicopters, no matter how reckless the pilots. Compared to life on the ground, it was like being up with the angels.

No sooner had we landed at Lashkar Gah than we heard the news about Osama bin Laden. It was the only topic of conversation, buzzing around the helipad. We walked through the heat and dust to the TFH office, where Colonel Lucas and his team were watching the news on Sky.

"So the witch is dead," I said.

"Quite," Colonel Lucas said.

I took a seat and watched the live footage from Times Square. Thousands of New Yorkers had come reeling out of their apartments in the early hours of a Monday morning, ready to celebrate. A lot of them bore an uncanny resemblance to drunken frat boys, pumping their fists and chanting "U – S – A" for the cameras. They'd taken to the streets at an incredible rate, their numbers growing all the time, presumably helped along by the naked triumphalism of the TV coverage.

"Do you think we need to issue a statement?" asked Meredyth, an unassuming captain who sat in the corner of the office. In charge of media planning, she was TFH's equivalent to Harriet.

"Not really," Colonel Lucas said. As the official spokesman for Task Force Helmand, he was required to issue statements about significant events in theatre (although this usually meant the latest British deaths). "I don't think it's for us to say anything. And I can hardly put out a statement before the Prime Minister has got out of bed."

He wasn't that excited about the news at all. None of us Brits were, really. Not as much as we should have been. The bastard who had triggered this entire blood-soaked adventure was dead – but to be honest, we all felt his time had passed. Most of us thought he had died years ago.

That said, some people thought he was still alive. Various rumours were already circulating around the base suggesting that bin Laden was holed up in a secret bunker on American soil, getting the full treatment from his interrogators. Some even suggested that he'd been captured more than a week ago, but the Americans had kept the news quiet so that it wouldn't get buried in all the coverage about the Royal Wedding. It didn't help that US authorities released conflicting accounts of his death in the days that followed, the White House backtracking on earlier assertions that bin Laden had died after engaging Navy Seals in a firefight.

"Bin Laden and his family were found on the second and third floor of the building," White House press secretary Jay Carney told reporters the following day. "There was concern that bin Laden would oppose the capture operation, and indeed he did resist. In the room with bin Laden, a woman – bin Laden's wife – rushed the US assaulters and was shot in the leg but not killed. Bin Laden was then shot and killed. He was not armed.

"We provided a great deal of information with great haste in order to inform you… and obviously some of the information came in piece by piece and is being reviewed and updated and elaborated on."

The news of bin Laden's death had initially broken on Twitter, fuelling the potential for misreporting. A thirty-three-year-old IT consultant called Sohaib Athar – who lived near the terror leader's compound in Abbottabad – had unwittingly told the world the first details of the Navy Seals raid. He was working late, writing code for a US company, when the noise of helicopters prompted his first tweets:

– Helicopter hovering above Abbottabad at 1 a.m. (is a rare event).
– Go away helicopter – before I take out my giant swatter.

It turned out to be a long night for Sohaib. His initial irritation soon turned to genuine concern when he realized the noise might presage something serious:

– A huge window-shaking bang here in Abbottabad. I hope its not the start of something nasty.

Meanwhile, in America, President Obama was making plans for a late-night announcement. Just before 10 p.m. the media were alerted by a tweet from the White House communications director Dan Pfeiffer:

– POTUS to address the nation tonight at 10.30 p.m. Eastern Time.

At this stage, reporters in Washington suspected the address would have something to do with bin Laden, but they did not know he'd been killed. That all changed at 10.25 p.m., when Keith Urbahn, an aide to former US Defence Secretary Donald Rumsfeld, tweeted the following announcement:

– So I'm told by a reputable person they have killed Osama bin Laden. Hot damn.

With Obama running late on his address (CNN reported he was writing it himself), anonymous sources at the White House started to confirm the rumours of bin Laden's death to the media. At 10.45 p.m., ABC, CBS and NBC all interrupted their schedules to break the news.

"We're hearing absolute jubilation throughout government," reported the ABC News correspondent Martha Raddatz.

The traffic on Twitter was now peaking at more than 5,000 tweets per second, at the time the third-highest rate ever on the site.* Finally, at 11.35 p.m., Obama went live on air to deliver his address:

"Good evening. Tonight, I can report to the American people and to the world that the United States has conducted an operation that killed Osama bin Laden, the leader of al-Qaeda, and

---

* The highest rate of tweets at that time had occurred at four seconds past midnight on New Year's Day 2011 in Japan, when users around the world sent 6,939 tweets, most of them wishing their friends "Happy New Year!" in Japanese. In comparison, traffic peaked at 3,996 tweets per second at 4 p.m. UK time during the Royal Wedding – NBC News (online), 3rd May 2011.

a terrorist who's responsible for the murder of thousands of innocent men, women and children.

"Today, at my direction, the United States launched a targeted operation against that compound in Abbottabad, Pakistan. A small team of Americans carried out the operation with extraordinary courage and capability. No Americans were harmed. They took care to avoid civilian casualties. After a firefight, they killed Osama bin Laden and took custody of his body.

"For over two decades, bin Laden has been al-Qaeda's leader and symbol, and has continued to plot attacks against our country and our friends and allies. The death of bin Laden marks the most significant achievement to date in our nation's effort to defeat al-Qaeda."

Regardless of what the US President said, everyone in the TFH office agreed that bin Laden was no longer the force he used to be. Ideology seemed to be slipping off the agenda.

"He's irrelevant," said Colonel Lucas. "This war is all about drugs now. We're fighting a narco-insurgency."

It depressed me to think bin Laden had already passed his sell-by date when the Navy Seals shot him up. We'd spent a decade trying to find him, scouring the caves and the foothills and the compounds, and now that he was dead, it didn't make a great deal of difference anyway. He'd been hiding for years in his reinforced lair in Pakistan while the War on Terror – or the war in Afghanistan, at least – had moved on. We couldn't just pack up and go home, leaving this country to its fate. We had to stay here and do the decent thing, carrying on the fight with the drug lords.

The other news of the day was that the poppy harvest was facing further delays – it would be another fortnight before the insurgents would be in a position to stash all their opium and pick up their weapons and explosives for the summer fighting season. This was a tiding that had a far greater influence on our battle rhythm than the death of bin Laden. We could expect a number of reprisal attacks in the coming weeks, but the real story was the drugs trade and its shifting calendar.

Heroin had an impact on everything, including the timetable by which we measured our successes. Senior officers didn't like to talk to the media about "winter gains" until all the poppy had been harvested. It was risky trying to describe the progress of the previous twelve months if the fighting season hadn't even started yet. Until you knew how hard the insurgents would come back at you, you didn't really know anything.

The death of bin Laden may have made all the headlines, but as a yardstick for success, it was a throwback to a bygone era. We'd long since given up measuring our progress by the amount of damage we inflicted upon the enemy: these days it was all about the number of our own troops getting killed. We could've done body counts on the Taliban – in fact, we did – but what message would that have sent to the media back home? *Hey, we're doing really well out here, wasting loads of Afghans.* The insurgents were getting killed all the time – it was like a turkey shoot. A far more persuasive figure could be derived from our own body count. If the rate at which we were dying was on the way down, then we must've been making progress.

Meanwhile, the injuries kept on coming. The number of British troops being flown into the hospital at Bastion was falling, but that didn't necessarily mean that things were getting better. Later that week the hospital released its monthly figures for April. Faulkner gave us the news at his evening brief.

"Three hundred and ninety-four casualties were treated for trauma," he said. "One hundred and fifty-two of those were Americans, and seventy-nine were Brits. Afghan Security Forces were fifty-five. Local civilians and other nationals made up the rest."

The British injury figure was low in comparison to previous Aprils, so we took some comfort from that, even though we all knew it was misleading. The Americans had replaced us in one of our most dangerous areas of operations – Sangin – where they were now starting to take casualties instead of us.

Faulkner also told us about the latest intelligence reports, suggesting that big splits were appearing in the Taliban's hierarchy. Fault lines were opening up between higher-level insurgents and the lower ranks, and also between young and old.

"Apparently the elders don't command the respect that they used to," he said. "A lot of the younger Taliban – when given orders – are saying, 'Why are we listening to these old guys?'"

If Taliban recruitment was still founded upon idealism – as it seemed to be back in 2001 – then I couldn't believe these youngsters would've answered back to their elders. Taliban was supposed to mean "religious student", but now they were also running a multi-billion-dollar narcotics business. A decade ago, the country made almost no money from heroin – now it was turning over around three billion dollars a year. In the midst of such a profitable narco-insurgency, was it any wonder if the latest recruits to the Taliban were less concerned about religious enlightenment and more interested in becoming drug lords?

A month after bin Laden's death, the Global Commission on Drug Policy branded the international war on drugs "a failure". The nineteen-strong panel, most of them former heads of state, argued that counter-narcotics strategies had cost hundreds of millions of dollars and caused thousands of deaths, with no evidence of any progress. They cited UN estimates that worldwide opiate use had risen by 35 per cent from 1998 to 2008.

The Global Commission's report made grim reading for those politicians who'd pitched the invasion of Afghanistan as a chance to fight not just terrorism, but also the drugs trade. In October 2001, three weeks after the destruction of the World Trade Center, the British Prime Minister Tony Blair told his Labour Party Conference the Taliban was exporting heroin to finance their military activities.

"The arms the Taliban are buying today are paid for by the lives of young British people buying their drugs on British streets," he said. "This is another part of their regime we should destroy."

Although this statement was true – 90 per cent of heroin being sold on Britain's streets at that time had come out of Afghanistan – the actual quantities involved were dwindling. In July 2000 the Taliban's leader Mullah Mohammed Omar – in collaboration with the United Nations – had banned Afghan farmers from cultivating opium, calling it un-Islamic. This had resulted in a massive drop-off in heroin production. Only 7,606 hectares of land in Afghanistan was used for growing poppy in 2001, a 91 per cent reduction from the previous year's estimate of 82,172 hectares. In Helmand Province itself, a traditional hotbed for opium, no poppy cultivation was recorded for the 2001 season.*

---

* United Nations Office on Drugs and Crime, *World Drug Report 2012*.

Dogs of War

Jumping onto a helicopter at Bastion sometimes felt like catching a bus, but really it was much more complicated than that. You couldn't pick and choose your flight time – it was randomly assigned and published in the daily flying programme the night before. That meant, in the planning stages for any given task, you had to set aside a day just to get to your destination, in case you were booked on an evening flight. The same applied for the journey back to Bastion, knocking another day out of the timetable. Thus it was that we spent a lot of our time in Afghanistan just sitting on our backsides.

We'd flown to Lashkar Gah on the morning of 2nd May for a job at the ANP training centre that wasn't due to take place until 4th May. Because the scheduling for road moves could also be unpredictable, 3rd May was given over to the twenty-minute drive between the two locations.

Lashkar Gah wasn't the worst place in the world to sit on your backside. It had one of the best canteens in Helmand, a NAAFI selling magazines, ice creams and cold drinks, and a well-stocked library in the welfare tent. Bizarrely, it also had a garden.

While Russ and Ali killed that first afternoon on their laptops in one of TFH's spare offices, I went over to the welfare tent to find something to read. The library consisted of hundreds of second-hand paperbacks, donated to the military by the British public. They'd been stacked chaotically on a series of uneven bookshelves that ran around the inside of the tent. Lee Child seemed to be the most popular author, the spines of his numerous bestsellers all faded and broken. His all-action hero Jack Reacher was obviously a big hit with the boys, despite being an ex-military policeman who'd spent most of his career banging up soldiers.

Clearly there was no accounting for literary taste. Fancying myself above all of that, I picked out a pristine copy of *Hangover Square* – apparently it was a modern classic – and walked over to the garden.

It was a curious parcel of land, crowded with flowers and greenery, looking very much like an allotment flown over from some English backwater. Surrounded by concrete walls, it felt entirely cut off from the rest of the base. A trio of Afghan gardeners normally tended to the beds, but right now I had the place to myself. I sat on a bench in the shade at the end of the garden and started to read my book.

I couldn't get into *Hangover Square* at all. Perhaps I'd only chosen it because I liked the title. The protagonist was apparently some sort of lunatic. I gave up after twenty minutes and took it back to the library, swapping it for *The Hard Way* by Lee Child.

I didn't go back to the garden, but returned instead to the office to check my emails. A frighteningly gaunt reporter from Agence France-Presse was walking out just as I arrived, called away on an impromptu job. She'd left her laptop in the office, her desktop showing a photograph of a burnt-out car on a desert highway with a dead dog in the foreground.

"Who would have a desktop like that?" I asked.

"A war reporter," said Ali.

I switched on my laptop. My desktop showed a picture of Monty – very much alive – sitting in my parents' kitchen, waiting for a biscuit.

I checked through my emails, then started on some research for the upcoming job at the ANP training centre. Recruits graduated from the centre every three weeks, but TFH was keen for us to record the latest passing-out ceremony ahead of the UK coroner's inquest into the notorious shootings at Checkpoint Blue 25. Our job was to capture footage and stills of newly trained Afghan police officers looking normal and non-psychotic, before distributing it to the British media in time for the opening of the inquest on 6th May.

I read through the media coverage of the Checkpoint Blue 25 killings, dating back to the incident itself on 3rd November 2009. The checkpoint had been built alongside a small crossroads just four hundred metres to the east of Shin Kalay, one of the most volatile parts of Nad-e Ali. Fourteen Afghan policemen lived and worked in the high-walled compound, theoretically enforcing the rule of law. They were supposed to control the road from Shin Kalay to the town of Nad-e Ali itself, but their presence had inspired a surge in violence. The Taliban had taken to attacking the compound almost every day, peppering its walls with small-arms fire, forcing the policemen to abandon many of their patrols.

At the height of the attacks in October 2009, the commanding officer of 1st Battalion Grenadier Guards, Lieutenant Colonel Charles Walker, had met with village elders in Shin Kalay to discuss the violence. This shura led to the establishment of a British mentoring team at the checkpoint, consisting of a dozen Grenadier Guards and two corporals from the Royal Military Police (RMP). They moved into the compound in the last week of October under the command of Regimental Sergeant Major Darren Chant, a former instructor at Sandhurst who'd previously served with the Parachute Regiment's elite Pathfinder Platoon. Noted for his height and build – a colleague had described him as a "man mountain" – he'd already distinguished himself on a previous tour of Afghanistan in 2007, carrying a young guardsman who'd just lost his leg in a bomb blast for more than a mile to a MERT landing site.

Most of the team at Blue 25 had been plucked from Lieutenant Colonel Walker's tactical group – police mentoring was not their area of expertise – but the soldierly discipline imposed by Sergeant Major Chant, along with the input from Corporals Nic Webster-Smith and Steven Boote from the RMP, produced immediate results. Within days of their arrival, attacks on the checkpoint had tailed off, and the Afghan policemen had returned to their duties.

One of the guardsmen, Lance Sergeant Peter Baily, told the *Daily Telegraph*:

"Even for the ANP, they were a pretty shoddy bunch. We turned up and were confronted with this bullet-riddled compound. The ANP were lounging around drinking tea. Not all of them wore uniform: they didn't seem to have any regular patrolling programme. Some slept in the compound, others in the village, and they seemed to come and go as they wanted.

"But the sergeant major got among them, imposed some discipline and began to work and nurture them, and they really responded. After a few days they were back in uniform and were patrolling with us every day. We were making real progress."*

On the afternoon of 3rd November, the team were chatting in the compound's courtyard with a number of their Afghan colleagues. Just back from a patrol, they'd removed their helmets and body armour and put their weapons to one side. They were sitting on a step that ran around the edge of the compound's main building, relaxing in the gentle sunshine.

---

* *Daily Telegraph* (online), 4th April 2010: 'Murder at Blue 25: British Soldier Speaks of Betrayal in Afghanistan'.

Suddenly one of the Afghan policemen, known only as Gulbuddin, stepped into the courtyard and opened fire on the soldiers with an AK-47. They were all lined up for him, and never stood a chance. Sergeant Major Chant was one of the first to be hit, along with Sergeant Matthew Telford and Guardsman James Major. Sitting near them was Lance Corporal Liam Culverhouse, who made a run for it.

"It just all went so fast," he said. "When he saw me, he just basically unloaded a magazine firing at me. He only managed to hit me six times, thank God."

Lance Corporal Culverhouse was hit in both arms and legs, and blinded in one eye.

Gulbuddin moved from the courtyard into the main building, still shooting. He hit eleven British soldiers in total – killing five – before fleeing the compound. The Taliban later claimed responsibility for the attack, although British commanders had suggested the rampage was more likely the result of a grudge. Gulbuddin himself was never caught.

A preliminary hearing into the killings at Blue 25 had already taken place on 11th February 2011. It was told that drug use was commonplace amongst the ANP, with Gulbuddin known to be a regular user of cannabis. Coroner David Ridley told the hearing in Trowbridge, Wiltshire: "There is a culture that the smoking of opium or cannabis is, to them, like to us the smoking of cigarettes."

The hearing was also told by Paul Kilcoyne, representing the families of Sergeant Telford and Guardsman Major, that drug use amongst the ANP was rife: "They would smoke drugs so they couldn't walk straight – and these are people with our weapons."

It was obvious the full inquest was going to paint a pretty appalling picture of the ANP. The preliminary hearing heard that more damning evidence was to come, detailing the ANP's penchant for skipping training, ignoring their mentors and sometimes refusing to go out on patrol. The deaths of the five British soldiers had made headlines around the world, so the inquest was likely to generate a fresh wave of negative press.

Against this backdrop, I had to find something positive to say about the ANP. The training centre on the outskirts of Lashkar Gah had opened just a few weeks after Gulbuddin's rampage at Blue 25, its launch brought forward as a result of the killings. Since December 2009 more than 3,000 recruits had graduated from the centre, completing an eight-week training programme that focused not only on policing skills, but also on reading and writing.* An eight-step vetting process had been introduced at that time, collating biometric and fingerprint information on each new recruit. Police pay had also increased, the monthly salary for a new recruit rising by a quarter to 8,250 afghanis – or about US \$165 – in the immediate aftermath of Blue 25.†

Drug abuse was still a problem, but the latest figures did at least suggest that things were getting better. In February 2009 the BBC obtained emails from an unnamed UK official who estimated that 60 per cent of Afghan police in Helmand were using drugs.‡ In March 2010 a report by the US Government Accountability Office found that up to 40 per cent of recruits in regional training centres were testing positive for drugs. Most recently, in January

---

*   Afghanistan has one of the highest rates of illiteracy in the world. According to figures released in May 2011 by Dr Jack Kem, the deputy to the commander of the US-led NATO Training Mission and Combined Security Transition in Afghanistan, 86 per cent of new ANA/ANP recruits were unable to read, write and recognize numbers – US Department of Defense news briefing (online), 23rd May 2011.

†   NATO (online), 28th November 2009: 'Afghan National Security Forces Announce Pay Increases'.

‡   These emails emerged following a Freedom of Information Act request put in by a BBC journalist to the Foreign Office – BBC News (online), 18th February 2009: 'Drug Abuse Hampers Afghan Police'.

2011, the commanding officer of the Police Development Advisory Training Team in Helmand, Lieutenant Colonel Adam Griffiths, said that over the past four months the number of new arrivals at the Lashkar Gah training centre who'd failed an initial drugs test had fallen from 8–10 per cent to less than 2 per cent.

Lieutenant Colonel Griffiths had quoted the figures in person at a briefing in Whitehall to an audience of journalists, but I couldn't find them reproduced anywhere by the British media (I only discovered them by trawling through the press archive on the MoD's official website). The 60 per cent figure was easy to find in the above-mentioned BBC report, as was the 40 per cent figure (most prominently on the *Daily Mail*'s website on 14th March 2010, under the headline "Nearly Half of Recruits for Afghan Police Fail Drugs Test"), but the 2 per cent figure proved elusive.

At a national level, of course, the media took no interest in good news for one very simple reason: it was *boring*. It didn't sell newspapers and it didn't boost the ratings. Only really terrible news could be relied upon to excite the people, so marketing our optimistic take on the ANP to the British media was going to be a struggle. My only hope of reaching a UK-wide audience was to persuade the bigger media outlets to run our coverage of the training centre as part of a companion piece to their coverage of the inquest. A then-and-now feature on the ANP, for instance, would give the story some added context and depth.

I wasn't holding my breath, however. The bigger media outlets didn't call on the Combat Camera Team for context and depth. They called on us for combat footage.

Fortunately, the smaller media outlets were a lot less discriminating. Working in local news, they had to be. I knew only too well the pain of trying to fill a bulletin with reheated stories about council cutbacks, the amount of chewing gum stuck to the city's pavements and the alarming rise in the number of pigeons shitting on park benches. I'd made a living out of it for ten years. Anything that was just a little bit different would get snapped up.

Out of curiosity, I searched for "Lieutenant Colonel Adam Griffiths" and found him on a couple of websites local to his home in Oxfordshire. He'd been interviewed by the *Oxford Mail* prior to his deployment – his photograph appearing under the headline "Army Officer Returns to Afghanistan to Train Police"* – and he'd also spoken to Oxfordshire's Heart Radio.[†] Because of his Scottish links – he commanded the Argyll and Sutherland Highlanders, 5th Battalion, Royal Regiment of Scotland (5 Scots) – he'd also been interviewed by the Glasgow-based *Daily Record* ("Scots Troops Fly out on Mission to Train 4,000 Cops in Afghanistan")[‡] and also the *Paisley Daily Express*,[§] based in the Argyll's recruiting patch of Renfrewshire.

Obviously local and regional[¶] news came with a reduced audience, but that was better than nothing. Lt Col. Griffiths had by now flown back to Oxfordshire and been replaced by Lt Col. Fraser Rea, the commanding officer of 2nd Battalion Royal Gurkha Rifles (2 RGR). Like his predecessor, he was based at Lashkar Gah in a tent just a few yards from the TFH office. Cornering him for an interview would be easy, but I also wanted to speak to his deputy, Major Paul Temple, who ran the training centre itself. In my opinion, he would make for the more interesting home-town story, being the man who lived and worked alongside

---

*   *Oxford Mail* (online), 7th October 2010.
†   Heart Oxfordshire (online), 6th October 2010.
‡   *Daily Record* (online), 15th September 2010.
§   *Paisley Daily Express* (online), 6th October 2010.
¶   Generally we regarded the Scottish, Welsh and Irish media as regional, rather than national, given the smaller population sizes.

the recruits. I couldn't find any pre-deployment interviews with him on the Internet, but that was probably because 2 RGR were normally based in Brunei, out of sight and out of mind of the British media. That in itself was no obstacle to a home-town story, of course – I'd simply target the media in the town he was born, pitching the story along the lines of "Local Man in Charge of Training the Afghan Police".

I met the man himself the following morning. Paul was a Manchester United fan with tattooed arms who'd worked his way up through the ranks over twenty-odd years, earning his wings with the Parachute Regiment along the way. He still wore the maroon beret – it sat comfortably above his sun-narrowed eyes – but the famous winged-cap badge had made way for the crossed *kukris** of the Gurkhas.

He gave us a tour of the training centre, steering us around a grid of humid tents and scorching ISO containers. It was a miserable place, with a noticeable lack of colour, as though everything had been bleached by the sun. I don't know why – maybe it was the lack of a gentle breeze – but the heat here felt different. It was like an invisible gel that clung to your skin, slowing down all of your movements. Even in the shade, it made you feel cranky and desperate.

Paul showed us a building site on a patch of wasteland within the compound walls, where a handful of Afghan bricklayers had started to build an accommodation block for the recruits.

"We've been given 1.4 million pounds to spend on this compound," he said quietly, as though this fact alone could get him arrested. For some reason, I wasn't sure he trusted us. What he thought we were going to do to him, I had no idea.

---

* Curved Nepalese knives, worn in miniature on the Gurkhas' cap badge.

He led us back to the cookhouse for lunch. On the way, we spotted a stray dog, sitting just inside of the compound wall. Being dog lovers, Ali and I called him over.

"Here boy!"

The dog walked towards us, panting happily, but as he got closer we saw that he only had one eye. He didn't seem to be in any pain – he was moving OK – but there was clearly something wrong. He came right over and sat down at our feet, looking up at us, showing us in close-up the huge gash running all the way down the side of his face, from his blood-caked eye socket to the corner of his mouth.

He clearly needed medical attention, but this was Afghanistan, so what hope did he have? There was a handful of British Army vets in theatre, but they were spread all over the place, and very much in demand. The only other option was the charity Nowzad,* but that would take time and money.

The dog looked at me, still panting happily. He seemed OK for now, but it was only a short matter of time before the wound would become infected. Flies were buzzing around his face in growing numbers, waiting to move in. I waved them away, wanting to comfort him, but reluctant to give him a pat on the head. I had no idea how he'd come to be injured, and if he bit me, I'd be bundled onto the next plane back to the UK for a long spell in quarantine, pumped full of anti-rabies drugs.

As though sensing my unease, the dog turned away from me, allowing me to stroke his back. I ran my hand along his thick coat,

---

* Nowzad was a UK animal charity set up in May 2007, named after a stray dog that Royal Marines from 42 Commando saved during a deployment in the town of Now Zad. The charity's main aim was to improve life for animals in Afghanistan, especially dogs. A lot of its donations were directed towards the rescue of stray dogs that had been befriended by British troops, helping them to find homes in the UK. The charity had also started to promote the use of humane options for dealing with out-of-control stray-dog populations.

the fur dark and matted with dirt. I wondered how he managed to cope in this heat.

"He needs to be shot," Paul said.

He was right, of course. Without immediate treatment, the dog was only going to suffer a slow, painful death.

I had assumed there would be someone on the base who did this kind of thing, maybe a corporal who'd been given five minutes of specialist training for this very eventuality, but I was wrong. Paul meant to do it himself, right now. He called the dog over and walked back towards the compound wall, removing his pistol from his hip holster. The dog followed, still panting.

Russ, Ali and I turned our backs. We heard the shots almost immediately – two of them, two seconds apart. I turned again and saw Paul already walking back towards us, grim-faced, returning his pistol to his holster. The dog was lying on its side, perfectly still, with no visible sign of injury. Paul clearly knew what he was doing. I had expected to see some blood on the wall, but it was still clean and white.

The coldness of it – the rendering of a friendly dog into a corpse – upset me, but at least he hadn't suffered. Paul had done exactly the right thing, dispatching him with the minimum of fuss, although that didn't make the scene any less depressing. For a minute or so, the world was just an empty, wretched place, with life nothing more than a futile exercise in the avoidance of pain.

We slowly made our way back to the cookhouse. Ali blew her nose, crying a little bit.

"I'm sorry, but he was suffering," said Paul. "I didn't like doing it."

In the cookhouse, the chef was refilling the trays at the serving counter, his red face glistening with sweat. The heat coming off the ovens behind him was off the scale. None of us were hungry, but we took some food anyway, Russ and I opting for meatballs and pasta, Paul going for pie and chips. Ali had hung back, taking a moment to compose herself in the transit tent where we'd left all our kit.

We sat at one of the tables in the dining tent. A few of the Gurkhas were still finishing their lunch, but most had returned to their duties.

"It must be unbearably hot in that kitchen right now," I said, trying to make conversation.

"Not as hot as if you're out on patrol in the Green Zone," said Paul, tersely.

We picked at our food in silence for a few minutes. Eventually Ali rejoined us, looking a little brighter. Trying to avoid the subject of the dog, we started to talk about the media. Paul seemed to think I was a press officer, for some reason.

"I'm actually a broadcast journalist," I told him. "Ordinarily."

"A *journalist*," he said, making no effort to conceal his disgust.

"I'm really just a newsreader," I said sheepishly. Persuading him to give me an interview was going to be harder than I thought.

The distinction was lost on Paul. He proceeded to launch into a rant about the evils of Fleet Street.

"What about all that phone-hacking?" he said, glaring at me.

I mumbled something about News International's appalling behaviour.* On the grounds of my being a journalist, he seemed to think I was personally involved in the scandal. I wasn't about to start an argument with him – he'd just a shot a dog – so I restricted my take on the matter to a few banalities. He stared at me, wanting

---

* Reporters at News International's soon-to-be-defunct *News of the World* having been found to have accessed the voicemail accounts of hundreds of celebrities and politicians. Later it was revealed they'd also hacked into mobile phones belonging to the relatives of British soldiers killed in action.

more, but I didn't give it to him. After a long moment he returned to his rambling monologue, bemoaning the state of the gutter press. I sat there in silence, prodding my meatballs with my plastic fork, waiting for him to run out of steam.

"So?" he said finally.

I snapped out of my meatball-induced trance. "So what?"

That glare again. "What newspaper do you read?"

"What newspaper?" I knew if I answered truthfully I would set him off again, but I couldn't be bothered to lie. "I read the *Daily Telegraph*."

"The *Torygraph*," he sneered. "And why do you read the *Torygraph*?"

It was a good question, even if it was dripping with contempt. I'd never really asked myself why I read the *Daily Telegraph*. Maybe I liked the plain writing, the like-minded editorials and the picture layout. All of that sounded about right, although it wasn't necessarily the most interesting answer.

"I read it because my father reads it." This was arguably true as well.

"Ah," he said. "So you're institutionalized."

I ignored this ridiculous but probably accurate comment. "What newspaper do you read?"

Paul took a moment to respond, giving it some thought.

"I read the *Independent*," he said finally.

"Right," I said. "Of course you do."

I wasn't buying it. Saying you read the *Independent* was like saying you were writing a book. All very worthy and impressive, but nobody actually did it. I tried to picture Paul with his head buried in the *Indescribablyboring*, but it didn't compute. The *Sun*, yes, but not the *Indy*.

Somehow we managed to get to the end of lunch without Paul shooting me. He returned to his duties while I joined Russ and Ali in the welfare tent, hoping to watch some TV. Unfortunately the air-conditioning wasn't working, so we crashed in the transit tent. It had eight bunk beds, all of them with proper mattresses and, most importantly, the air-conditioning was working. The three of us had plenty of room; the only other occupant being a dog-handler called Alan. He'd brought his dog in with him, a black-and-white springer called Memphis.

"He's four years old," said Alan. "This is his fourth tour."

Fourth tour. Poor old Memphis. He looked exhausted, like a dog three times his age. Four tours in four years was outrageous. He should've been back in England, with grass under his paws, not sand. I gave him a scratch behind the ears, looking into his big droopy eyes.

Oh Memphis, what are we doing here?

At that point, to my amazement, he growled at me. I'd never been growled at by a springer before. I was confused and a little bit unnerved, a combination that triggered all sorts of questions. What was wrong with him? What was wrong with me? Could he tell where my hand had been? Did he know I'd been stroking another dog, just seconds before its death?

I had always been a great believer in the psychic capabilities of dogs. Monty and Trudie, my mother liked to assure me, would always start barking precisely five minutes before my arrival on the doorstep at home. What was that, if it wasn't a supernatural gift?

Memphis stayed with us in the tent that night, lying on the bed alongside his master's legs. Despite his fondness for growling, it was good to have him there, snoozing on his little blanket. He brought to mind a catalogue of images from a more comforting world, evoking long walks in the countryside, muddy boots on the porch and foamy pints of bitter by the fire. I fell asleep to the sound of his gruff breathing, wondering whether he was happy or sad, wondering whether he dreamt of Afghan fields or English meadows.

We filmed the police graduation ceremony the following morning. Memphis did his thing, sniffing around the ISO containers that surrounded the parade square, looking for any suspect devices. Security had to be tight, with a dozen Afghan dignitaries watching the ceremony from a row of seats on the front edge of the square. In the middle of this audience was Helmand's Chief of Police, a beefy character called General Hakim Angar. Around 150 recruits took it in turns to march across the square to collect a graduation certificate from him. He would've made a nice big target for any would-be assassins, but thankfully none of the recruits felt the need to start off their careers by killing the boss.

I interviewed him after the ceremony. We needed his input for some all-important "Afghan face". Despite his busy schedule, he was more than willing to stop and talk, his interpreter rendering his Pashto into a number of media-friendly soundbites for my press release.

"This was a very good ceremony," he said. "I can see the recruits are very disciplined and they'll be very good at their jobs. When they go back to their checkpoints and their neighbourhoods, the people will see they've got a professional police force."

Paul meanwhile was saying nothing. Having made vague assurances about giving us an interview at some point during our stay, he'd been doing a very good impersonation of a man who was trying to avoid being interviewed at all costs. Whenever an opportunity arose to say a few words, he'd found something else to do, something more important. At lunchtime, with our transport about to return to Lashkar Gah, I tried to corner him one last time, but he couldn't get away from me fast enough.

"He doesn't like doing interviews," said Ali, who'd managed to have a couple of normal conversations with him. "He thinks of it as grandstanding."

In the end I interviewed Paul's boss back at Lashkar Gah, Lieutenant Colonel Fraser Rea. We met him outside the Gurkha temple (more of a tent, really) next to the TFH office, just after its inaugural service. He had a red dot in the middle of his forehead and a purple flower behind his ear, but they soon came off. The notion of grandstanding was not a concern, and he was happy to answer a few questions.

* * *

Back at Bastion, we learnt that the Checkpoint Blue 25 inquest had again been put on hold. It would now take place later in the month. Regardless, Russ still edited his footage, Ali still collated the best of her photographs, and I still wrote up a couple of press releases for national and regional media in the UK (Lieutenant Colonel Rea was originally from Scotland). TFH had said they would now be responsible for marketing the content, so once we'd done all the cutting and polishing we sent it over to them for distribution.

With all that done, we had a couple of empty days in our schedule. This meant loitering in Bastion, waiting for our next job. Consequently I spent a fair few hours at my desk, trying to look busy. This was no easy task, and the time would drag, but it was worth hanging around just to marvel at some of the characters that occasionally strayed into the office.

At one point a rather large, matronly naval officer walked in, returning a camera she'd borrowed from Ali. She was a practice nurse from the hospital's Primary Healthcare Department. In her spare time she would visit Bastion's handling facility for detainees,* giving our guests there some moral support. She wrote poems about them, and had tried – and failed – to get permission to photograph them.

"Some of them are not very pleasant people," she said. "But some of them are quite chatty."

As for the war itself, that seemed to be on hold. Evidently the insurgents were still preoccupied with the opium crop. The main item in Faulkner's brief that evening concerned our food supplies.

"You may have noticed a lack of choice in the cookhouse recently," he told us. "It's because half a delivery of protein – in other words, meat – and pudding went bad in transit. So two planes carrying 150 tonnes of pudding and protein are being lined up. Until then, we may have to use some US supplies, so expect lobster tails."

The following day was equally slow. I went to the gym in the morning, returning to the JMOC after lunch. Time seemed to stand still at about 3 p.m., so with no interesting characters coming into the office, I offered to drop off some paperwork at the hospital.

Walking over to the hospital's reception, I passed the entrance to the Emergency Department. One of the Afghan cleaners was hosing down a gurney on the concourse, sending a stream of blood into the nearby drain. So much for a lull in the war. I dropped off the paperwork at the front desk in reception and then walked over to Heroes. My predecessor Sean had advised me to take a moment for myself every now and again, just to collect my thoughts (this was surprisingly erudite, coming from Sean). With so much time on my hands, I'd started thinking about Omid Haft, the big operation that was coming up at the end of the month. It was making me a little nervous, so now I wanted a distraction.

---

* I.e. the camp prison. The detainees were mostly suspected Taliban.

In Heroes I bought a can of Diet Coke and a glazed doughnut, handing over two dollars to the bored American at the till.

"Bad for you, those doughnuts," he said.

"I'll sweat it off."

I sat down at a table in the corner. There were about half a dozen soldiers in the room, all of them sitting in silence, captivated by a television infomercial for sports bras. A line of blondes were parading across the screen in just their underwear. The camera kept zooming in to each model's chest, highlighting the bra in all its glory.

The advert was over all too soon, replaced by some crappy action movie. I drank my Diet Coke and ate my doughnut, feeling pretty distracted.

I toyed with the idea of another doughnut, but thought better of it. I had to stay in some sort of shape. Omid Haft promised to be a hard slog. We'd be out on the ground for at least a week. I couldn't afford to be carrying any excess weight.

There I was, thinking about Omid Haft again. I wasn't supposed to be doing that. It would only lead to thoughts of death and horror. *Actual* death and horror, as opposed to the hysterical antics being played out on the television.

I left Heroes and went for a piss, using one of the Portaloos near the cookhouse. I could've walked back to the JMOC and used the Portakabin toilets – they were a hundred times cleaner and more civilized – but I didn't want to go back towards the office just yet. That would only lead to introspection, which would lead to the dark side. I wanted to do something else, something different, so I decided to give the Portaloo experience a try. How bad could it be?

It was like stepping into an oven that baked nothing but loaves of shit. Apart from the fact that it stank, the heat was ridiculous

– almost comical. I started to sweat within seconds of closing the plastic door. This was no longer a time-killing distraction – this was a very real form of acclimatization training. I flicked up the toilet seat with my boot and had my piss as quickly as I could, taking in the graffiti-covered walls as I relieved myself.

The graffiti fell into two categories: soldiers slagging each other off, and soldiers crowing about their imminent departure. On my right, there was a whole chain of messages from the former, most of them centred on the great Paras-versus-Craphats debate:

– All Paras are dumb fucks
– Fuck you, craphats! Dumb? I'm a Tom with a degree and what the other lads lack in Quols make up for with common sense and tactical awareness. Craphats are solid!
– Fuck off, you cocky set of pricks
– U all envy us Paras
– TO ALL PARAS. Your not special! I did a jump once. 25 ft out of your mums bedroom window

And so on. At the foot of it all, someone had settled the debate with:

– Ross Kemp is harder than all you wankers!

As for the graffiti on my left, there were a couple of messages that caught my eye:

– I'm outta here in less than 7 hours
– Are you flying home tonight for end of tour? No, must be me! Enjoy this shithole…

I finished my piss and wandered back to the JMOC, wondering what it would be like to be one of those soldiers going home. I was now almost halfway through my tour, with another ten weeks to push. It wasn't a long time on paper, but in my head it seemed like an eternity.

At the brief that evening, Faulkner said it had been another quiet day. In lieu of any major incidents, he gave us another round of intelligence updates and parish notices.

"The Taliban have finally worked out what the balloons in the sky are for,"* he said. "So they've started moving more at night to avoid the cameras. They're also telling the locals that we're using the cameras to spy on women."

As propaganda went, it wasn't a bad line from the Taliban.

"One more thing," Faulkner said. "The Dog Section has put out a call for volunteers to go over there and help walk the dogs. Apparently they need a hand keeping them exercised."

Naturally I volunteered. What else was I going to do? Stay in the office and go mad?

I walked over to the Dog Section the next morning. It was not difficult to find. A giant paw carved out of wood hung on the metal fence outside the office. I went inside and introduced myself to the sergeant major behind the desk. He was a short, intense man who took his job very seriously.

"You mustn't let the dog misbehave," he said. "They can't afford to pick up bad habits."

I'd always been totally pathetic with dogs, allowing them to get away with anything. This was going to be a new experience.

He led me outside to the kennels. Dozens of dogs – springers, Labradors, Belgian shepherds – sat in wire cages, barking at us.

---

* Persistent Ground Surveillance Systems, like the one at Shahzad. Most of the larger bases had them.

"Which one do you fancy?" he asked.

"I've always been rather partial to springers."

The sergeant major showed me a small black springer who was very lively, bouncing around inside his kennel, barking his head off.

"This is Dave," he said.

"Good name."

I took Dave out alongside a handler who was exercising a Belgian shepherd. We walked out of the kennels onto a long stretch of enclosed desert, barren except for the odd bit of scrub every twenty yards or so. Dave was straining on his lead like a dog possessed, trying to chase down some invisible entity just beyond his nose. The temptation to let him go was enormous – I felt sorry for him – but I knew that would be wildly inappropriate. Instead I kept jerking him back on his lead, trying to get him to heel.

Dave only ever paused for breath when we passed a bit of scrub. Then he would go into his urination routine: he would cock his leg and pee on the scrub from one angle, then he would turn around, cock his other leg and pee on it from a different side. Then he would turn around again and pee on it for a third time from the original angle.

I began to wonder whether Dave had obsessive-compulsive disorder. He repeated this routine at least a dozen times during our thirty-minute walk. Then to cap it all off, he did a very runny shit on the last bit of scrub before we got back into the kennels.

Even in a war zone, you were supposed to pick up the dog poo. The sergeant major had given me a little plastic bag just before we set off. I looked down at Dave's mess, dripping off the scrub. It was an impossible task.

"Don't worry about it," said the handler. "You'll have to let that one go."

I was worried about Dave – he seemed stressed. I could recognize the symptoms. I wasn't urinating in a weird way just yet (OK, apart from the Portaloo episode), but I could relate to his situation: sitting in an office/kennel all day, thinking/barking for hours on end, then going out into a hostile environment for an uncertain spell, before coming back and repeating the process all over again.

Man or beast, it was always going to make you go a little bit strange.

Embeds

Reporters came through the JMOC all the time, but the start of the summer brought with it a larger than usual influx of journalists and producers. Eighteen of them were due to arrive at Bastion on the evening of 19th May, the most high-profile being Ross Kemp and the *Sun*'s Defence Editor Virginia Wheeler.

Ordinarily, they would've all completed an RSOI training package upon arriving in theatre, but the powers that be back in the UK (the JMOC answered to Permanent Joint Headquarters – or PJHQ – based at Northwood) had decided that was no longer necessary. It was considered too time-consuming, with the package for those deploying outside the wire lasting five days. If a reporter was only in theatre for two weeks, it meant almost half their embedment was taken up with training.

"Instead they'll get a day-long ad-hoc safety brief from some corporal," Faulkner complained. "It's all wrong. There are huge issues with safety. We can't just send them out there without the proper training."

It wasn't just a question of training, either. The need for acclimatization was becoming increasingly evident. The daily highs in Helmand were now in excess of 40°C. On 14th May, Op Minimize was called for a heat injury – a British soldier had collapsed while out on patrol. It was lifted again a few hours later, but it showed that bullets and bombs weren't the only things that could hurt us.

More heat casualties were flown into the hospital at Bastion the following day. Three members of 4 Scots had gone down in Nahr-e Saraj. They were brought in behind three Royal Marines from 42 Commando, who'd also been out patrolling in the same district. They didn't have heat injuries – they'd triggered an IED. Two of them had fragmentation injuries to the eye and arm respectively, while the third Marine – later named as nineteen-year-old Nigel Mead – died of his wounds.

That afternoon I helped our admin sergeant to sort out some of the body armour that would be distributed to all the embeds coming at the end of the week. His name was Mick, and he was our equivalent to Tom, the lumbering commando at TFH. Mick was a little lighter on his feet than Tom, blessed with a quick wit and a lively sense of humour. He was originally from Jarrow, a fact you couldn't help but be reminded of whenever he opened his mouth.

"I'm no Geordie," he would say. "I'm a Mackem."

"Mackem?"

"That's Sunderland to you, sir."

The spare body armour was stored inside an ISO container next to the office. We sorted through all the different sizes, dripping with sweat in the sauna-like heat.

"That Virginia Wheeler is coming," Mick said, wiping his brow. "From the *Sun*."

"So I've heard," I said. "Is she nice?"

"Is she nice? She used to be a Page Three girl."

"What?" This was news to me. "How old is she?"

"Twenty-seven? Twenty-eight?"

It seemed highly improbable to me that Virginia Wheeler was an ex-Page Three girl, but I still went back into the JMOC and googled her. I managed to find a few byline shots of her, but nothing to suggest that she used to take her clothes off for a living. Mick was either misinformed or just pulling my leg.

Still, she was attractive enough, and certainly easier to look at than Ross Kemp.

I saw one of her stories in the *Sun* later in the week. It was taken from a press release that Dougie – still bored out of his mind in charge of Strategic Messaging – had come up with.

GOATS GO AWOL

BRITISH troops in Camp Bastion have been put on special alert – to hunt down three GOATS that have gone AWOL from the base.

The trio escaped from the army training village under cover of darkness. The farm animals – code-named Tom, Dick and Harry – are part of the realistic Afghan training village on the military base where the troops practise drills.

Colour Sergeant Roughley, of 1st Battalion, the Grenadier Guards, said: "While we are impressed with the goats' skills, it's time to return to duty."

Whether the goats would return in time for Virginia's arrival remained to be seen. Either way, her stories for the *Sun* would soon be heading into much darker territory. Op Minimize had been called yet again, for the third day running. Five British soldiers had been taken to Bastion with heat injuries, all of them collapsing before 10.30 in the morning. Later that afternoon, an RPG attack near a patrol base outside Lashkar Gah caught three British soldiers, leaving them with blast injuries. The following day in the same area, three soldiers from 3 Mercian – our hosts at the Royal Wedding celebration – suffered blast injuries after their armoured vehicle hit an IED.

As the temperature rose, so did the operational tempo. Virginia would get a few days in theatre to find her feet, then she'd be outside the wire for Operation Omid Haft. She was getting embedded with 42 Commando, and would be joining foot patrols throughout the operation.

My own preparations for Omid Haft, meanwhile, were not exactly going to plan. I still hadn't managed to meet up with the elusive Afghan Combat Camera Team. We'd arranged to start their training in a classroom at Shorabak a week earlier, but none of them had turned up. Even Mikkel had failed to appear. We didn't hear from him until the following morning, when he'd cycled over to the JMOC to apologize.

"I am very sorry," he said in his long-suffering Scandinavian way. "They were unable to make it."

I didn't press Mikkel for their excuses. Like he'd said before, it was the Afghan way. We just had to be patient and go with it.

We finally met up with the Afghan team on 17th May, just a week before Omid Haft was due to start. The four of them – a major, a captain and two NCOs – were waiting in one of the empty Portakabins when we arrived. Mikkel introduced everybody (with the help of an interpreter) and we got started straight away. Russ and Ali split them down into pairs and took them through the basics of filming and photography, while I took a few pictures in the faint hope this auspicious occasion could be turned into a story. The Afghans were a bit glassy-eyed at times, but generally they seemed to follow what Russ and Ali were saying. The two NCOs were the most keen to learn, while the two officers, perhaps wary about the presence of Ali (a woman telling them what to do) were more stand-offish. Either way, no one fell asleep or stormed out, so the day was judged a success.

When we returned to Shorabak the following morning to continue the training, we were greeted by the sight of Mikkel outside the Portakabin. He was sitting on a bench in the shade, rubbing his sweaty temples.

"Morning Mikkel," I said.

He looked up at me and smiled, all wry and careworn.

"Good morning, Christian," he said. "As you can see, they are not here. They have all been given other jobs by their commanders." He shook his glistening head. "I think we'll have to call today a write-off."

We went back to the JMOC and spent the rest of the day doing not very much. Op Minimize was called again at just after midday, so I killed some time on Ops Watch. I was beginning to find its unquestionable authority strangely reassuring, in a comforting "this is what the fuck is going on" kind of way.

Also, its format reminded me of the old BBC teleprompter that used to give out the football results on *Grandstand* on a Saturday afternoon.

In Nahr-e Saraj that morning, about a dozen insurgents had attacked a foot patrol from 1 Rifles with small-arms fire and RPGs. Two Apaches were called in, firing eighty rounds of 30-mm ammunition and a Hellfire missile. One insurgent was killed, and a member of 1 Rifles was shot in the buttock.

Meanwhile in Musa Qala, a Georgian patrol had driven over an IED containing 5 kg of explosive. Two of their soldiers had been flown into Bastion with blast injuries.

An Afghan child had also been flown into Bastion after stepping on an IED in Sangin. The child had lost a leg below the knee, and was left with a "mangled arm".

Ops Watch also reproduced the details for some of the many "significant acts" that took place across the rest of the country every day. Helmand was just one of thirty-four provinces in Afghanistan. It was easy to forget that we Brits occupied just a tiny portion of this vast landscape. I scanned through the lists of events that had taken place elsewhere that day.

In Takhar Province, about a thousand demonstrators had gathered in the centre of Taloqan District to protest over an ISAF operation in which four Afghans, two of them women, had died. The crowd had turned violent outside the Governor's compound and the local ANP headquarters. The ANP had fired live ammunition at some of the protestors, who fled and laid siege to the nearby Provincial Advisory Team headquarters instead. The German soldiers inside, under a barrage of petrol bombs and small-arms fire, also started shooting back. According to the initial estimates, twelve Afghan civilians had been killed and seventy-two injured. Ten ANP had been wounded, along with two Germans.

In Kandahar, a joint patrol from the ANA and the US 502nd Infantry Regiment had discovered 2,000 kg of hashish in Zharay District. The ANA had burnt the drugs on site. They were then engaged by small-arms fire and RPGs from an unknown number of insurgents. One US soldier was killed and one wounded.

In Wardak, a patrol from the US 3rd Squadron 89th Cavalry Regiment had discovered a weapons cache in Maidan District. It contained twenty-seven 122-mm rocket engines and two 107-mm rockets. An Explosive Ordnance Disposal (EOD) team had conducted a controlled detonation of all the munitions. The resulting explosion blew out the windows of two nearby houses, injuring two Afghan children.

In Zabul, a vehicle patrol from the ANA had driven over an IED in Shah Joy District. Three ANP had been pronounced dead at the scene. Two injured ANP had been flown to the hospital at Qalat, where they'd died of their wounds.

In Paktika, a joint patrol from the ANA and the US 506th Infantry Regiment had been engaged by small-arms fire from two insurgents in Mota Khan District. They returned fire, and following the engagement discovered the body of an eleven-year-old boy. A six-year-old boy was also wounded during the incident. The local elders were angry and blamed ISAF for the death. It still wasn't clear whether the dead boy had been firing at the patrol. The KIA (Killed in Action) was listed as "suspected insurgent". An investigation had been launched.

In Kunar, a patrol from the US 2nd Battalion 35th Infantry Regiment had been engaged by small-arms fire from an unknown number of insurgents in Darah-ye Pech District, resulting in one wounded US soldier. An F-15 from the 389th Expeditionary Fighter Squadron had then come in and dropped a 2,000-lb bomb, forcing the insurgents to break contact.

In Nangarhar, a car bomb had exploded near the Jalalabad Customs House in Behsud District. It had targeted a bus filled with ANP instructors and students. Eleven ANP were killed and six wounded. The blast also killed eight civilians and wounded twenty-two.

Other than that, it was a quiet afternoon – not untypical, by Afghanistan's standards. Terrible stuff happened all the time, spread out in pockets across the country. Here at Bastion, we were well out of it, removed from it all. The reports came in, and the casualties came in, but the insurgents never troubled us. We were working on a space station in the desert. No one was going to get to us out here. You could fly your granny in for tea and not worry about it. We were completely safe.

Omid Haft

The IDF attack on Bastion on 19th May – the first of its kind for eighteen months – took place just hours before the arrival of Ross Kemp and Virginia Wheeler, but no one told them about it, or indeed any of the embeds. It wasn't the kind of information they needed to know, so we all kept quiet. They'd find out sooner or later – somebody on camp was bound to let it slip – but at least they wouldn't hear it from the JMOC.

While Ross Kemp was eating his fruit-and-raisin bars at the training village the following lunchtime, there was another little media crisis in progress at the JMOC. There'd been a cock-up with Virginia Wheeler's timetable – she was supposed to be flying straight out to Lashkar Gah to interview a brigadier, but Dougie had misread the programme, and she'd unknowingly missed the flight. Frantic efforts were now under way to reschedule the interview. Flights to Lashkar Gah were supposed to be booked at least four days in advance, so finding her another seat was not going to be easy.

To make matters worse, Dougie had disappeared. He'd crept out of the office after details of the cock-up had emerged, and three hours later was still missing. A search party consisting of Mick and Ali took the minibus and went out to look for him.

They soon found him. He was wandering around the vigil site, right next to the JMOC. A section of desert the size of two football fields, it was the best escape from cabin fever that Bastion had to offer.

"I've had enough of this place," he told Ali. "I've got to get out of here."

Faulkner's rhetoric was clearly lost on Dougie, but you couldn't hold that against him. His role in charge of Strategic Messaging had devolved into something trivial and undemanding. He had become a glorified media handler, a babysitter to reporters passing through Bastion. Despite his lofty job title, he had no actual job. Strategic Messaging meant everything – and therefore nothing.

I had a chat with him the following afternoon, back in the office, hoping to cheer him up. The Virginia Wheeler situation had been resolved – she'd managed to get another flight to Lashkar Gah earlier that morning – so at least her timetable was back on schedule.

"Good news about Virginia," I said to him.

"Yes," he said quietly. "Now we've just got Ross Kemp to sort out."

"He's not causing problems, is he?"

Dougie stared at me blankly. He looked exhausted.

"He was due to go on a Sea King this evening," he said eventually. "But now he wants to go on a Chinook."

"Why a Chinook?"

"It's his favourite helicopter."

To be fair, this wasn't as daft as it sounded. The Chinook was much more filmic, much more symbolic of the war, than the Sea King. Ross was flying out with his team to join 45 Commando at one of their patrol bases. Any footage from the flight could well end up in the opening shots of his new TV series, so it had to look good.

Dougie wasn't entirely in agreement with me on this one.

"There's a war on," he said. "We can't just move it around to suit Ross Kemp."

Ross did eventually get his Chinook, which was probably just as well. His team was carrying an enormous amount of kit – over twenty bags and cases – so they'd have struggled with the much smaller Sea King (unless they'd kicked everybody else off).

Over the next two days, as I waited to deploy on Omid Haft, the inquest into Checkpoint Blue 25 took place. With nothing else to do, I spent a lot of time at my desk, reading through the coverage. Predictably, all the newspaper headlines were focusing on the drugs problem, with Gulbuddin's behaviour in the run-up to the killings attracting most of the media's attention. One of the guardsmen, Paul Steen, had told the inquest he'd been out on a previous patrol with Gulbuddin and noticed that he had been smoking cannabis.

"One time I was on the Northern Sanger* alongside the ANP, and he was sat next to me and he was smoking cannabis," said Steen. "It is easy to recognize the different smell between a cigarette and cannabis. I reported it to the Sergeant Major. He was quite sleepy on that Sangin duty. He could hardly walk straight. He was armed."

The inquest also heard from Lance Corporal Namarua, who was badly injured in the incident. He told the court he "didn't trust" the ANP.

"My general view was that I was not happy, to be honest," he said. "Sleeping in the same room together, I was not happy with that. I didn't trust them. The feedback that I got [from superiors] was supposed to be: work with them – and we were supposed to be able to bond. I can't explain why I could not trust them: it was just a feeling that I could not suppress."

I looked through all the British media's coverage of the inquest, dovetailing into the wider issue of ANP recruitment, but I couldn't

---

* A watchtower on the base's perimeter. Bastion had hundreds of them, but most checkpoints and patrol bases only had two or three.

find any of the material we'd recorded at the police training centre in Lashkar Gah. TFH had taken on the responsibility for its marketing, but all I managed to locate was a short film of the graduation ceremony on Armyweb. We had been hoping our material would appear on a much bigger platform, but sometimes it didn't work out that way.

I just hoped that our footage and stills from Omid Haft would find a wider audience. Nobody wanted to risk their life for a photograph or a film or an interview that was going nowhere.

* * *

We caught a Chinook to Patrol Base 5 for Omid Haft on the afternoon of 24th May. Russ and Ali were both excited about the operation, and even I was starting to feel more upbeat, riding the high from the adrenaline boost that came with every helicopter trip in Afghanistan. I told myself it was time to stop fretting about worst-case scenarios and just go along with the whole fucking carnival. There was no point wasting your precious time on this earth just lingering on the sidelines, shitting yourself.

At Patrol Base 5 I met our point of contact from the Brigade Advisory Group, a very tall officer from Devon called Captain Foot-Tapping. This put me in an even better mood. With someone like Foot-Tapping on our side, we couldn't possibly fail. His name had that ring of eccentric British invincibility that immediately inspired confidence. He even spoke like a toff. His ancestors had probably conquered half of India. We were going to win this war after all!

Foot-Tapping went through some of the details with me. We'd now be going out in two days' time, in the early hours of the morning, timing our departure to coincide with the 1 Rifles/42 Commando heli-insertion 5 km north of us. Russ, Ali and myself would be attached to a mixed company* consisting of eighteen British soldiers from the Brigade Advisory Group and sixty soldiers from the ANA. Our patrol would be moving very slowly, all of us in single file, following in each other's footsteps. We'd lay up in a compound about 2 km outside Patrol Base 5 on the first night, then complete the rest of the move up to Salaang by the following evening.

"At Salaang you'll get the chance to do a few interviews," said Foot-Tapping. "And hopefully the Engineers will get the all-clear to build the bridge."

For us, the bridge was the main event. Russ and Ali would get plenty of footage and stills of British soldiers out on patrol – framed wherever possible with Afghan soldiers in the same shot – but we still needed to show the British public what it was their boys were actually trying to achieve. We weren't just out here looking for a fight – we were here to build bridges, in this case literally.

We stayed at Patrol Base 5 that night. I slept badly, kept awake by the nearby mortar line, firing illumination missions into the early hours. They stopped at around 2 a.m., allowing for a small window of calm, before waking us all with a rousing blast at 5 a.m.

I went for breakfast at 6.30 a.m., joining Russ and Ali at one of the tables in the dining tent. None of us had slept well.

"Did you hear the bang?" asked Russ.

"You mean the mortars?"

"No, a Husky hit an IED outside the base."

"That's why the Apaches are up there," said Ali.

Two of them were circling the base, omniscient in the cloudless sky. They were scouring the ground for insurgents while the Engineers recovered the Husky. The driver and passengers had all

---

*   Known as a *tolay*.

walked away from the blast, reinforcing the vehicle's well-earned reputation for safety. Chunky and robust, it was designed for saving lives.

It turned into another stupidly hot day. Temperatures were now hitting 42°C. With nothing else to do, I spent the afternoon reading a book on my camp cot, wearing just a pair of sweat-soaked boxer shorts, staying out of the sun. We'd opened up both ends of our little tent, but it still felt like a sauna, the heavy canvas doing nothing to dissipate the heat. By dinner I'd drunk four litres of water and was still thirsty.

After dinner a vigil was held for Colour Sergeant Kevin Fortuna, the soldier from 1 Rifles who'd been killed by an IED two days earlier near CP Sarhad, barely a kilometre from where we were all standing. Everyone on the base – there were about a hundred of us – formed a hollow square by the two flagpoles near the dining tent. By now the sky had clouded over, and the wind had picked up. A number of officers and senior NCOs read out prayers and eulogies, struggling to make themselves heard over the noise of the Brigade flags, still flapping wildly at half-mast.

We had an early start the next morning, getting up at 02.30. Once again I got very little sleep, but I felt OK, waking up to the faint sound of distant helicopters. I put on my Bergen – it was heavier than I would've liked, but perfectly manageable – and walked with Russ and Ali to the meeting point by the back gate. We could see lots of other guys already there, getting their kit ready in the darkness, visible by their issued head torches. They looked just like miners preparing for a descent into the underworld.

"We've got a delay," I heard one of them say. "Moving off at 0430 hours."

That gave us another hour. I didn't know if there was some sort of problem, but I was grateful for the slippage. It started to get light at 4.30 a.m., which meant it would be easier for the point men to spot any IED ground sign. We did have night-vision goggles, but they weren't exactly high-definition.

That said, we were less likely to get shot in the dark.

I walked back to the dining tent to get some cold water, bumping into Foot-Tapping on the way.

"It's still too windy for the heli-insertion," he said, his silhouette looming over me. Dozens of illumination rounds had been fired into the night sky behind him. "They're just waiting for it to calm down a bit."

I could still hear helicopters in the distance, so someone was flying. In the dining tent I took out as much water from the wardrobe-sized fridge as I could carry, returning to Russ and Ali with my arms full of 500-ml bottles. They were sitting on their kit by one of the ISO containers near the back gate. I handed out the water, and we started drinking.

I was just opening my second bottle when a soldier came over and introduced himself. I couldn't see his face in the darkness, but his voice told me everything I needed to know about him.

"I'm Colour Sergeant Fisher," he growled. "You'll have to give us a hand with some of our kit."

He passed me one of the reserve Vallon metal detectors and a 66-mm rocket launcher. Russ and Ali had already declined my offer to carry some of their kit – they insisted they'd be OK – so I did have some spare capacity. I strapped both items onto my Bergen, hoping I wouldn't be called upon to use them.

Eventually we got going, the wind dying down enough for the heli-insertion to get the all-clear. It was closer to 5 a.m. as we walked out of the gate in single file, Russ, Ali and myself at the rear, with the stocky Colour Sergeant Fisher – looking as tough as he sounded – covering all our backs. Above us the murky clouds had formed a protective blanket, keeping out the sunshine. We knew it wouldn't stay that way for long, but for now the weather was perfect.

The ANA were waiting for us along the track, spread out in single file. There must've been about a hundred of them, all out in the open. They shuffled forward after a few minutes, moving very slowly. The first kilometre of the route had already been cleared of IEDs, but they still took their time. The Afghan commander, a chubby man who refrained from wearing a helmet, kept moving up and down the line, muttering to himself. Every time the troops at the front stopped, we all got down on one knee. If we were stationary for more than a couple of minutes, we'd sink back onto our Bergens, giving our shoulders a break. I was carrying around 45 kg of kit, body armour included. Some of the men in our patrol were carrying in excess of 60 kg.

It took us two hours to reach CP Sarhad, just a kilometre north of Patrol Base 5. It was a holding area, giving us a chance for a break. We all rested up against Sarhad's mud walls while Foot-Tapping went through the orders again with the Afghan commander. Some of us chatted, some of us smoked, and some of us ate snacks. All of us drank water.

We set off again about thirty minutes later. The clouds had yet to break, and we still had the breeze to keep us cool. A narrow track took us into a much greener landscape now, the thick grass coming up to our waists. It was still a disconcertingly obvious route, so we left nothing to chance, stopping constantly. The ANA had their own Vallon man up front, but we also carried out Vallon checks in their wake.

It took us three and a half hours to move from CP Sarhad to our next lay-up point at Compound 43. The distance was roughly one kilometre. Every man was now drenched in sweat. The midday sun was out and the breeze had disappeared.

Foot-Tapping had hired the compound from a local farmer, providing us with shelter for the rest of the afternoon and the night ahead. We carried out Vallon checks on the outer walls, then moved inside. There was a well, an orchard and a number of empty stables. We would be sleeping in relative comfort tonight, before leaving at first light.

We split the compound between the ANA and ourselves. Each stable measured about ten feet by twenty feet – big enough for a section of men. We cleared spaces for our roll mats on the crumbling mud floor, kicking aside all the straw and dried chicken shit. Dust billowed up towards the thatched ceiling just a few feet above our heads, where dozens of bees tended to their own comforts, seemingly oblivious to our presence. They'd built a network of little hives, each the size of a clenched fist.

We spent most of the afternoon inside, avoiding the sunlight. The walls were almost two feet thick, keeping out the worst of the heat. I was sharing my stable with ten other soldiers, Russ among them. They were mainly from 3 Mercian, although a few came from 1 Rifles. Two of them came in following a short patrol around the compound, their Dorset accents filling the stable.

"We've just been chatting to one of the elders," said one of them. "There are two IEDs out there."

The devices were dug into an alleyway alongside the compound. The elder had pointed them out to the soldiers, who'd marked them for the EOD team. It was troubling to think what could've happened if the elder had said nothing, but also reassuring to know that some of the locals were ready to help us out.

We all took turns on sentry duty. The lookout point was on the corner of our mud roof. To get there, you had to climb up a ladder and crawl over to the edge of the building. You couldn't walk on the roof, in case it collapsed. Whenever the sentries changed over, dragging themselves into position, bits of mud and thatch sprinkled down from the ceiling onto our heads. After I'd stopped worrying about the two IEDs, I started worrying about the beehives, wondering whether they would fall down onto our heads as well.

I went on sentry at 3.30 p.m., crawling across the roof to get my handover from one of the young Mercians. He pointed out my "arcs" and then talked about the three "fighting-age males" wielding hand scythes in the field to my front, about a hundred metres away. They'd been cutting wheat for the last hour and weren't deemed a threat, but I still had to watch them.

They did nothing of any interest. They just carried on cutting the wheat. I lay on the corner of the roof in the sun, feeling like a lizard. The temperature was still in the thirties, but the lack of exertion meant the whole experience was actually quite pleasant. Like being on holiday. It was nice to get outside, away from the bees and the crumbling ceiling. There was a gentle breeze blowing across the wheat, keeping me cool. Beyond the farmers were trees and green fields. It was like a postcard from Tuscany.

At just after 4 p.m., an IED detonated. It was to my right, but I could only guess at the distance. One kilometre? Two kilometres? Three kilometres? It was impossible to say. I certainly couldn't see anything.

Colour Sergeant Fisher called up to me. He was manning the radio in a small pocket of shade in the main courtyard.

"You see anything, sir?"

"Nothing, Colour Sergeant."

No information was forthcoming about the explosion. We kicked our heels in the compound for the rest of the afternoon, then gathered in one of the stables for a briefing after dark.

According to the elders, the Taliban had fixed our position and were planning to attack us the next day. "But they're just rumours at this point," said Foot-Tapping, studying his notes by torchlight. "Besides, we're going to be leaving at 5 a.m."

There was still no word on the afternoon IED, but overall the operation seemed to be going well. There had been only one minor casualty during the earlier heli-insertion, a soldier from 1 Rifles suffering a broken leg after a partial IED detonation. Otherwise it had been very quiet. An interpreter had been injured after a grenade had been fired into another compound, but that was about it.

Foot-Tapping rounded off the brief by once again reminding everyone to treat the compound with respect. "Make sure you pick up all your rubbish before you go," he said. "We might have to come back here one day."

"How much is this place costing us?" someone asked.

"We've given the owner 10,000 afghanis."

"What's that?"

"A couple of hundred dollars."

"I want to see the management," said one of the Dorset soldiers.

"Too right," said another. "The roof is falling in."

Those of us not on sentry went back to our kit and tried to get some sleep, but it was a lost cause. The sentries were doubled up after last light, crawling across the roof in pairs. The noisy changeovers, along with all the bits of crap falling from the ceiling, made for a restless night.

Reveille was at 4.30 a.m., just as it was starting to get light. Nobody bothered trying to cook any breakfast. We just packed our kit, cleared away the odd bit of rubbish and formed up in the courtyard. The ANA were up and about as well, and we all set off together at just after 5 a.m.

The plan was to get to Salaang by dusk. It was just under two kilometres away, but as before we were allowing ourselves plenty of time. The ANA led the way and we followed on behind, negotiating a stream and a couple of harvested poppy fields before stopping on a track about four hundred metres short of a compound at just after 7.30 a.m. We planned to lay up at the compound and finish the journey to Salaang in the afternoon.

We sat on the track for another three hours, warming up in the sun. There was no shade, and nothing to hide behind. Young men on motorcycles would occasionally drive by, making us all sit up, but otherwise it was quiet.

The owner of the compound eventually let us in at 11 a.m. It wasn't as nice as Compound 43 – there was cow shit everywhere – but it did have a clean-looking stream running through it. I had run out of water by now, and was more than ready for a drink. The stream water itself was not to be trusted, but one of the Mercians lent me his Lifesaver,* allowing me to refill all my empty bottles without fear of infection. I poured a sachet of blackcurrant powder into one of them and gave it a try.

It tasted fantastic. I emptied my bottle in two swigs, and did it all over again.

---

* One of the best bits of kit in Afghanistan. A bottle with an internal filter, it allowed you to purify water in seconds. You filled the bottle's inner chamber from the stream, then pressed down on a plunger (much in the manner of a coffee machine), forcing the water through a filter into an outer chamber, ready to be drunk.

Once again, we took turns on sentry. One of the Mercians sat on the roof in the atrocious heat and gazed out across the fields, while the rest of us stayed in the shade. The compound had just one empty stable to protect us from the sun – many of us had to pin ourselves to the perimeter wall, sheltering in a band of shadow two feet wide.

I went on sentry later in the afternoon. Another IED went off. Again, I couldn't tell how far away it was, but that didn't matter. It came in over the radio.

"It was just over three kilometres south-west of us," said Colour Sergeant Fisher. "Must be the Marines."

It was most likely 42 Commando, the unit hosting Virginia Wheeler. If she was out with a patrol, she would've been at the back, theoretically the safest place. We'd only heard a second-hand-contact IED report at this stage. There was no word as yet on any casualties.

We all left the compound at just after 5 p.m. We had about another kilometre to get to CP Salaang. By now the sky had started to cloud over, and a gentle breeze had returned. We made good time across the open fields, keen to get into Salaang before nightfall.

Salaang was a checkpoint that was in the process of being upgraded into a patrol base. Ordinarily it was home to a platoon, but right now there were around seventy British troops and almost two hundred Afghans. Everywhere you looked, soldiers were trying to make themselves comfortable, sitting on their kit, drinking water, smoking cigarettes and cooking rations. We eventually found some space on the edge of the vehicle park, close to a JCB digger that was emptying gravel into a line of Hesco containers. It was dusty and noisy, but at least it was somewhere to lie down. We marked out a sleeping area with glow sticks – hoping that no one would drive over us in the middle of the night – and then got a small fire going.

We had another impromptu briefing that evening. Foot-Tapping was busy on a separate tasking with the ANA, so another officer from the Brigade Advisory Group, Captain Chris Ball, took us through the main details.

"It's thought the insurgents have been overmatched in our area," he told us. "We think they've pushed out towards the south and the west."

"What happened with that IED?" asked someone.

"Two dead from J Company, 42 Commando," he said. "Three injured."

There were no sentry duties for us that night. We laid out on our roll mats and drifted off to sleep under the stars, grateful that none of us had been blown up.

The next day we built a sun shelter out of stakes, wire mesh and tarpaulin. At a push, a dozen of us could squeeze in underneath it. It wasn't the greatest piece of engineering in the world, but it stopped us from burning up. We sat in our priceless shade and chatted, read books and smoked. Someone appeared with a twenty-four-can pack of iced tea, and it all felt remarkably civilized.

I was reading a book called *Chickenhawk* by Robert Mason. It was about the experiences of a US helicopter pilot in the Vietnam war. Each page I turned fell out in my hand, the glue in the spine having melted. I'd promised Ali she could read it after me, so I had to fold up every loose page and keep it in my pocket.

Mid-afternoon, news came through that J Company had hit another IED, very close to the scene of the previous day's explosion. There was no word yet on casualties. Meanwhile the commanding officer of 1 Rifles, Lieutenant Colonel James de la Billière, had come under fire while driving alongside the Nahr-e Bughra Canal. His party – consisting of four armoured vehicles – had only been travelling for a few kilometres, but they still managed to draw small-arms fire on four separate occasions.

At just after 5 p.m., with the sun low in the sky, the Royal Engineers started to build the eagerly awaited bridge outside Salaang's back gate. All the ground overlooking this section of the canal had been cleared of insurgents in the first few days of the operation, allowing the engineers to work in relative safety. It was the first time they'd ever tried to erect a forty-four-foot unreinforced bridge in an operational theatre, making it a historic occasion. There were about a dozen of them, crawling all over three huge vehicles parked up on the bank. They had to extend a launch rail slowly across the canal from one of the vehicles, establishing a platform on the opposite bank (it looked like a giant fishing rod, with a metal stand on the end). They could then start sliding into place the main parts of the bridge, which consisted of lengths of aluminium alloy weighing two tonnes each. If all went according to plan, the entire structure would be up and ready in less than two hours.

Russ and Ali moved among the engineers, recording their progress, while I chatted to their commander, Major Ralph Cole.

"This bridge is vitally important," he said. "It'll mean our troops can easily move north of the canal and disrupt the insurgents up there. It'll also open up a trade route for the local Afghans."

"Once the bridge is nearly done, I'd like to interview you in front of it," I said.

"Of course," said Ralph. "It shouldn't take too long."

By now the end of the launch rail was resting on its stand on the far side of the canal. The engineers were starting to manoeuvre the first lengths of aluminium alloy into position. We watched as two of them stood over the middle of the canal, balancing on the metalwork. With the threat from insurgents kept to a minimum, the only real danger came from the canal itself. The two men still had to wear their body armour and helmets, which meant a fall into the water could easily result in them both drowning, weighed down by the very kit designed to save their lives.

Suddenly the stand on the far bank buckled and collapsed under the weight of the launch rail. Tonnes of metalwork bounced violently up and down. The two men on the rail bounced up and down with it, but somehow managed to hang on. They inched their way back towards the safety of the near bank as the rail's originating vehicle creaked and groaned, threatening to flip over.

"I'll do that interview another time," said Ralph tersely. "Excuse me."

He hurried over to join his men on the bank. They were running around frantically, trying to work out what the hell had gone wrong.

Russ was still filming, so I went over to join him. He had managed to record the whole debacle, standing less than twenty feet away.

"Should make for a good training video," he said.

A breathless sergeant ran towards us. For some reason, he'd only just noticed the camera.

"You can't show this," he blurted. "It's a massive fuck-up."

"It's OK," I said. "We're Media Ops."

"We're not here to make anyone look bad," said Russ.

By now it was gone 7 p.m., and getting too dark to film anyway. Russ, Ali and I walked back to the vehicle park while the engineers continued to work into the night, securing the launch rail so they could have another go in the morning.

The vehicle park was teeming with life, most of it Afghan. They'd set up a huge cooking pot over a fire, throwing in countless chopped onions and chunks of chicken. The smell from the pot drifted across our sleeping area, making us all yearn for a good curry. Our rations were good, but not that good. A dozen Afghans stood around the fire, their faces lit up by the flames, waiting for the feast.

Captain Chris Ball came over and gave us another brief, mosquitoes flitting in and out of his torchlight as he went through his notes.

"As you may already know, J Company hit another IED today," he said. "They've got two down, injured. Another IED went off near PB5. That was the ANA. A group of them left the base to get some food from a nearby village, taking a vehicle down a short cut that was known to be unsafe. None of them are dead, but the vehicle is a write-off. The ANA at PB5 are refusing to recover it, so our guys are having to get it.

"We've been having a few problems with the ANA," he went on. "Some of the Afghans with J Company are now refusing to soldier because of the IED threat. Here, you may also find there's some drug use going on. There's not a great deal we can do about it. Just be aware of it."

After the brief, we stretched out on our roll mats, chatting about home. It was always a good time to reminisce just before bed. You went back to your happy place, got nice and relaxed, and drifted off. Before long, a sweet-smelling smoke hung over the sleeping area, helping us all to unwind. It came from the Afghans over by the cooking pot, relaxing after their feast.

"Can you smell ganja?" I heard Chris Ball say.

"Yep," someone else murmured.

We all slept well that night. Without any sentry duties to worry about, most of us got at least seven hours. We didn't start getting up until 5.30 a.m., by which time it was broad daylight. Ali got a little fire going, and we all had some coffee and heated up some boil-in-the-bag rations.

The engineers had to wait for spare parts to arrive from Bastion, and weren't due to resume work on the bridge until 8 a.m. To fill the time, Russ and I interviewed two brothers from the Brigade Advisory Group. Lee Swain was a rough-hewn sergeant major who was helping the Afghans with their logistics, while his younger brother Paul – a slightly more fresh-faced staff sergeant – was passing through the base with another *tolay*.

"Having a brother out here gives you that reminder of being back home," said Lee. "It means you can talk to someone that's very close to you about the situations you've been through. It's very helpful."

"It's good to work alongside him," added Paul. "I don't get to see him all that often, but every few weeks we meet up. It's good to have a chat and see how he's getting on. That side of it makes life a little bit better out here."

"And how does the rest of your family feel about you being out here?"

"They've got mixed feelings," Paul said. "There's the worry that we're serving in a country like Afghanistan, but they're also quite proud that we're both out here. We're fortunate to be in touch with family and friends on a regular basis, so it's nice to let them know that we're OK."

Russ filmed them working alongside each other, unloading ration boxes from the back of a lorry. It was all staged, but we had to get them doing something together in the same shot.

"That's fine," I said after a couple of minutes. "Thanks for that. Have a safe tour."

"Cheers, sir," said Lee. "You too."

By now the engineers had gone back to work, so Russ and I joined Ali at the bridge. The launch rail was back in place, and the whole thing was taking shape. We took some more footage of the engineers in action, then I interviewed Major Cole.

"Have you deleted that footage from last night?" he asked me.

"No, I've put it on the Internet."

He looked horrified. "What?"

"I'm joking. It's not going anywhere."

"Thank God for that." He gave out a long sigh, then had a thought. "Actually, could we get a copy of it?"

"Of course."

With the bridge filmed and photographed, our work on Omid Haft was done. We walked back into the base, picked up the rest of our kit and said goodbye to the Mercians. They were sorting out kit themselves, getting ready to go out on patrol.

"Can't sit around here all day," said Colour Sergeant Fisher. "Work to be done."

We managed to get a lift over to Patrol Base 2 with the Commanding Officer of 1 Rifles. He'd come to Salaang for a meeting, and was now heading back to his headquarters. His four vehicles were covered with bullet marks. We climbed into the Mastiff at the back and waited for the rounds to start pinging off the armour.

We got to Patrol Base 2 in twenty minutes – no one shot at us. From there, we got a lift to Patrol Base 5, which was almost deserted, save for the inexplicable presence of Mikkel. We saw him coming out of the gym, dripping with sweat.

"Christian, good to see you again," he said, wiping his brow.

"Mikkel, what are you doing here?"

"I'm trying to find the Afghan Combat Camera Team."

We had dinner with him. The cookhouse was near empty – most of the Marines on the base were out on patrol – but the chef knocked up some beef stir fry. After five days of rations, it tasted superb.

"The Afghans, I don't know," said Mikkel, picking at his food. "They keep disappearing. They went off yesterday to film a meeting of elders. I don't know when they'll be back."

We all had an early night, going our separate ways before 8 p.m. I was sharing a tent with Russ. He watched a DVD on his laptop, while I tried to sleep. A group of Marines were sitting outside the next tent, just in from a patrol. They chatted and laughed in the moonlight. Morale seemed pretty high.

At about 9 p.m., yet another IED went off. Impossible to say how far away it was, but it was loud. The Marines stopped laughing, and to a man they all said the same thing:

"*Fucking hell.*"

There was a pause, then the Marines carried on chatting. We'd know soon enough how close it was. The Ops room would send word, and the Marines would be put on standby.

No word came from the Ops room. The IED must've been far, far away. The Marines started playing cards and laughing again.

* * *

We flew back to Bastion the next morning. Harriet was waiting for us at the helipad. We threw all our kit into the back of the minibus and she drove us to the JMOC.

"Phew," she said. "I think some of you might need a wash."

I didn't make it into the office for another hour, needing no extra encouragement to have one of the longest showers of my life. Russ and Ali still had all their footage and imagery to edit, but I just needed to write up a few press releases. We had three and a half hours on the UK anyway, with our material bound for local stations and papers in the West Midlands (following the Mercians) and South-West (the home of 1 Rifles and 42 Commando). We were also targeting the national stations, although the lack of combat footage would make it a tough sell.

I checked through all my emails before starting on the press releases. My inbox was filled with all the usual flotsam, although one message did stand out. A US Media Operations officer had asked TFH for any footage and stills showing transition and progress in Afghanistan. Colonel Lucas had copied me in to his reply, which started as follows:

Apologies for the late reply. I have just been out on the ground doing a media-escort job with one of the UK's national newspapers. They wanted to get into a "contact" with the insurgents and I managed to get them into several.

I pondered the remarkable irony of Colonel Lucas's email for a short moment, then read through Virginia Wheeler's coverage of Omid Haft. She was the only UK journalist covering the operation. I soon found her report in the online version of the *Sun*, posted a day earlier:

The *Sun* has seen the true hell of war in Afghanistan at close range – patrolling with hero Royal Marines as a massive Taliban bomb killed two legendary commandos.*

The report focused on the deaths of Marine Sam Alexander and his troop commander Lieutenant Ollie Augustin. They had been patrolling in Loy Mandeh, a Taliban stronghold. Lieutenant Augustin was

---

* *The Sun* (online), 30th May 2011: 'When the Taliban Shot at Our Patrol, J Company Saved us… Then I Heard Bomb Blast That Killed Two of those Brave Marines'.

leading his men through a village compound when the IED deto-nated. Embedded with Colonel Lucas in a separate troop, Victoria had heard the blast from a mile away. As the news of casualties came over the radio, she noted the reactions of the Marines around her:

One commando, on his second tour in Afghanistan, sat with his head in his hands, shuddering: "Please let this not be another Sangin."

No sooner had I finished reading the article than Virginia herself walked into the office, carrying her laptop. There were no spare Internet connections in the crowded reporters' tent. Dougie had suggested she come into the JMOC. She took a seat at the spare desk and got to work.

We all spent the rest of the day in the office, although the work tempo started to drop off around mid-afternoon. Virginia didn't say much about Omid Haft, but her presence did inspire a cer-tain amount of debate about newspapers, with Faulkner leading the way. He monitored the British newspapers for stories about Afghanistan, and had just spotted a story in the *Daily Telegraph* about fears for the mental health of bomb-disposal experts.

"People die all the time doing IED clearance," he said. "Let's do a mental-health survey of bomb-disposal experts. Are they a) all right or b) mentally fucked up?" He shook his head. "Can someone take a common-sense pill?"

Virginia smiled at his little outburst. "You heckle us journalists, don't you?" she said. "How high am I on the list?"

It was good to have her in the office. She wasn't supposed to be there, but that didn't matter. She was a beautiful, articulate war reporter – she could go anywhere she wanted.

She was back in the office the next day, this time for a phone interview with Michael O'Neill from the Helmand Provincial Reconstruction Team (PRT) at Lashkar Gah. As the Head of Mission, he oversaw many of the local reconstruction projects, leading a 200-strong team of civil servants and service personnel.*

The interview lasted about twenty minutes. Virginia said goodbye and then hung up with a sigh.

"How did it go?" asked Faulkner, leaning back in his chair. "I noticed you didn't do much talking."

"It's the third time I've interviewed him," she said, shaking her head. "You cannot get a word in edgeways. He likes to talk, and he likes to talk very fast. And I just can't get him to talk to me in plain English. If I was writing for the *Guardian*, it would be fine, but I'm writing for the *Sun*."

The readers of the *Sun*, it seemed, were a tough sell when it came to stories about transition and progress.

"Your average Brit will say: we're building this entire country, we've got massive economic problems, unemployment through the roof, the life expectancy in Glasgow is less than it is in Haiti. Against that background, it's hard to write stories about breast-feeding programmes in Afghanistan. Michael said, 'It's all about Afghanistan.' But if you publish that comment, even in the *Independent*, you'll still get comments like 'What about Britain?'"

She flicked through her notes. "I need to make a link between breast-feeding programmes in Afghanistan and security. How am I going to do that? The British public struggle to disconnect the military side from the advanced level of infrastructure building."

"It's not sexy," Faulkner said. "A guy with a rifle is sexy."

---

* Michael O'Neill's multinational PRT was roughly 60 per cent civilian, 20 per cent military/police and 20 per cent Afghan. He co-ordinated stabilization and development work across Helmand in conjunction with ISAF and the government of Afghanistan.

"Well no, it's not that. It's just that it's hard for them to grasp the finer points of government policy in a country they see as a huge problem."

Dougie tried to help by emailing Michael O'Neill's office and asking for some more concise quotes that the *Sun* could actually use. Some more quotes duly came back, but they still weren't up to the required pithiness.

"They just don't get it," Dougie said, staring forlornly at his computer screen.

While this little drama was being played out, I took a call from Captain Luke Price. He handled press matters for the Brigade Advisory Group.

"Did you do an interview with two brothers from the Brigade Advisory Group?" he asked.

"Yes, I did," I said. "We've just started the editing."

"Could I ask you to stop?"

"What's happened?" I sat up.

"One of them got hit by an IED."

"Oh my God. Is he OK?"

"He's going back to the UK with his brother," he said. "Minus his left arm."

"Christ…"

There was a pause, then Luke spoke again.

"We do have other brothers in the unit," he said. "We've got some guys in B Company."

"OK," I said slowly. "I'll get back to you on that one."

It was Paul who'd been injured. We saw Lee in the coffee shop a couple of hours later. He spoke to us for about five minutes. He seemed relieved to be able to talk about it to someone. He'd been cooped up inside the hospital for hours.

"It's a depressing place," he said. "We want to get out of there now." They were due to fly back to the UK at midnight.

"I agree," said Ali. She'd recently spent a day in the Emergency Department, taking clinical photographs at the request of the hospital. "Two hours is enough."

I'd never really thought of the hospital at Bastion as a depressing place, but then my reasons for being there had never been that depressing. It was a shining beacon of hope and civilization from one angle, and a meat house full of maimed soldiers and bloodied civilians from another.

The *Sunday Mirror* had just published extracts from a short diary written by a surgeon who'd recently served at the hospital. Lieutenant Colonel Mike McErlain had been working as a consultant orthopaedic and spinal surgeon. He was back home now, so the content had been cleared UK-side. The paper's headline was pure tabloid, referring to Bastion as "Camp Hell", but the diary itself was quite powerful. Just the first week sounded bad enough, and he was on duty for two months straight:

DAY THREE

An Afghan soldier has been blown up by an IED. His leg is so badly injured it can't be saved. It is a grim task. An American surgeon puts on rock music in the background of the operating theatre. There's no room for emotion as you fight to save as much of them as you can.

DAY FIVE

My first double amputation. The sight is pretty shocking. We all try to do as much as we can for him and keep him alive.

DAY EIGHT

Three amputations from three separate incidents make this one of the hardest days of my life.

I am exhausted afterwards as I struggle with the adrenaline coursing round my system. I sit and think it is such a shame. One is a dad who'll never play football with his kids again. But keeping these guys alive is important.*

* * *

I went to the hospital the next morning for less traumatic reasons – I needed some anti-malaria tablets. I'd run out weeks before Omid Haft and forgotten all about them. Foot-Tapping had been loudly reminding his men throughout the operation to keep taking the tablets (although I found it hard to imagine Colour Sergeant Fisher worrying about malaria), so now I was back at Bastion, I thought it best to get some more. I followed the signs to the Primary Healthcare department – just down the corridor from the operating theatre, but really a million miles away – and made myself known to the nurse on reception.

"When did you last take your tablets?" she asked.

"About a month ago."

"Have you been out in the field since then?"

"Yes."

She looked horrified.

"Only for about a week," I added.

"You should still have taken your pills."

"I also drank stream water, but I used a Lifesaver bottle."

"The Lifesaver bottle won't stop malaria."

---

* *Sunday Mirror*, 29th May 2011: 'Camp Hell Diary: An Army Surgeon's Searing Account of Treating Soldiers on the Afghanistan Frontline'.

She left her desk and went into another office, then came back and told me that the doctor in charge was astonished by my stupidity. She handed me a box of Paludrine tablets and a box of Avloclor tablets. She also gave me a Malaria Warning Card, which I was supposed to carry in my wallet for the next two years. It said I might have been exposed to MALARIA, which MUST be considered in case of fever.

"I do spend a fair bit of time here at Bastion," I told her.

"Bastion is non-malarial," she said. "We've had about one case in the last ten years."

"Great." That sounded more like it.

"There are seven types of malaria in the field, and these pills protect you against two of them."

"OK." So pretty useless then.

I went back to the office. It was quiet that morning. Virginia and her photographer Andy were packing up their kit, getting ready for their flight back to the UK later that afternoon.

"She's a bit upset," Dougie said. "TFH have told her they're not happy with one of her stories."

Virginia had been chasing a story about one of the search dogs on camp, a Labrador called Fizz who'd swallowed a plastic duck. The duck hadn't come out, so Fizz had gone under the knife. A surgeon had freed the bird, and Fizz had been able to return to duty. It was a funny, feel-good story, offering an alternative to all the misery coming out of Afghanistan. What made it perfect was the X-ray picture of Fizz's stomach, clearly showing the duck trapped inside. The *Sun* readers were going to love it.

Unfortunately, TFH didn't like the story. Someone in their office thought it made the search dogs at Bastion look incompetent. Because TFH had originally coordinated Virginia's visit, they were responsible for clearing her stories rather than the JMOC. According to Dougie, they weren't prepared to clear this one unless Virginia dropped the X-ray picture.

"If you take the funny picture out, what's the point?" he said. "The *Sun* won't run it."

The *Sun* never did run it. TFH wouldn't budge. They were happy to clear a report on Omid Haft that raised the prospect of "another Sangin" and never once mentioned the ANA. That was fine. Not a problem.

But a short item about a duck-swallowing Labrador? No way. Not a chance.

That would make us all look incompetent.

PART THREE

The Retreat to Kabul

Two days after Omid Haft, we flew to Kabul to film the launch of the ANP's District Commander's course. The top police officers in Afghanistan were starting five weeks of specialist training, led by officers from across the UK. A diplomat called Scott met us at the airport and escorted us to the British Embassy, our home for the next two nights.

"Have you eaten?" he asked. "I can order you some pizza."

It was 10.30 p.m., and we were all hungry.

"Sounds great," I said.

We sped through the empty streets of Kabul, listening to Scott put in an order for three large margheritas on his mobile phone. The usual traffic that stymied the route from the airport had died away for the night. Only the pavements showed any signs of life: men of all ages loitering in the doorways of grimy eateries, chatting and smoking.

"Is sixty dollars OK?" said Scott.

"Sixty dollars?" said Ali. "Are these pizzas coming from Italy?"

"That's fine," I said. "I'll get these."

I didn't want to upset Scott, because I was hoping he'd be able to rustle up some booze as well. The Embassy was famous for its relaxed stance on alcohol, and I hadn't drunk anything for almost three months.

"You got any beer, Scott?" I asked.

Twenty minutes later we were sitting on Scott's couch, drinking Heineken and eating pizza. He lived in a villa in the leafy grounds of the Embassy compound. Eight other staff lived there, sharing a large lounge and kitchen. It was like a student hall of residence, but with a better-stocked fridge.

"That's one thing the Foreign Office does well," he said. "We arrive somewhere, sort out the supply of alcohol, and then have a look around."

The three of us nodded, gorging on our pizzas, the Heineken never far from our lips.

"I'm going to get my head down," he said. "You've got your room keys. I'll see you at breakfast."

"What time are we off?"

"Transport leaves at 9 a.m.," he said. "We never go out before then."

"Why not?"

"Bad things tend to happen between 7 a.m. and 9 a.m."

"Not a problem," I said. "See you in the morning."

The timings were extremely civilized, and had there been more than ten cans of Heineken in the fridge, we would've almost certainly got drunk. The three of us stayed on the couch and drank for another hour, before retiring to our rooms – double beds, fresh sheets – for eight hours of untroubled sleep.

The absence of a hangover made it much easier to cope with the Kabul traffic the next morning. It was the usual crawl, although this time through a part of the city I hadn't seen before. Our route to the Staff College took us past the dusty windows of the famous Shah M Book Co., which inspired the 2003 bestseller *The Bookseller of Kabul*.

"I'd love to have a look inside," Scott said. "I go past it three or four times a week."

"Why don't you?" I asked.

"You don't just pop out to the shops in Kabul," he said. "I could go inside, but why take the risk?"

The Staff College was hidden from the main road by a wire-mesh security fence screened with tarpaulin and topped with razor wire. Inside the front gates the manicured grounds came as a pleasant surprise, dotted with cedar trees and gazebos. We parked outside a set of office buildings to the back of the compound and walked into the main headquarters. The Afghan police officers had just sat down for their first lesson in one of the air-conditioned classrooms on the top floor. An officer from Northumbria Police was taking them very slowly through the principles of the course, giving the interpreter alongside him a chance to unravel his Geordie accent.

"There are some big challenges in this country," he told them. "Corruption is one of the biggest problems you're going to face. But we're going to make sure you've got the best chance of success out there."

We interviewed him afterwards. He was one of the most sun-tanned Geordies I'd ever met.

"I love it out here," he said. "The sun is always shining, and the money is fantastic."

"How long is your contract?" I asked.

"Two years. But I'm extending."

All the other British officers wanted to extend as well. We interviewed three of his colleagues, two from Kent and one from Hampshire. None of them wanted to go home. None of them wanted to return to the lower pay and the indifferent weather.

We stuck around for lunch, waiting to catch the Afghan officers during their break. Scott brought us crisps and sandwiches, and gave us some bad news.

"The Afghan colonel that runs this place won't let you interview anyone on the course."

"Why not?"

"I have no idea. But I'm going to find out."

It took him twenty minutes to come back with an answer.

"He wants a colour printer," he said. "Absolutely unbelievable."

"Does he need a colour printer?" I asked.

"No, not really. But I'll have to get him one anyway."

Eventually I was allowed to interview four of the Afghan officers. They were all in their mid-thirties, but each of them looked about fifty. Like a lot of Afghan men, their faces alone could've told any number of stories. They had brown eyes that seemed to be full of dark wisdom, as though they'd seen the most terrible things. Ali took dozens of shots as they answered my questions about the value of the training and the importance of the Afghan police. They spoke slowly and carefully, with a gravity that felt like it had been earned through years of suffering.

With all our interviews done, we returned to the Embassy. It was Saturday night, and the diplomats in the villa next to us were throwing a party. Classical music drifted out of the French doors that had been opened up to the garden. The first guests were starting to arrive: bright young things carrying bottles of wine, laughing and joking as they walked across the grass in the twilight.

We wandered over to the Embassy bar. It was a bit farther away, next to the outdoor swimming pool. Ali lit a cigarette and sat with Russ at a table near the water's edge. I went into the bar and came back with two beers and a gin-and-tonic.

"I didn't know you smoked, Ali," I said.

"I'm trying to give up."

"Is it the stress of Afghanistan?"

"That's right, boss," she smiled. "It's very stressful here."

We sat in silence for a moment, each of us lost in our thoughts. I started to think about home, walking Monty and Trudie at dusk. It was my favourite time of year for dog-walking: the wheat would've just been cut, opening up all the fields, letting the dogs run wild under a harvest moon.

Suddenly the evening call to prayer cranked up from the mosque next door. It was a tremendous wailing, emanating from the minaret which overlooked the Embassy compound.

"Perfect," said Russ.

Two Embassy staff were sitting at the table next to us. "It used to be much worse than this," said one of them. "They used to have a really screechy PA system, with loads of feedback. So we bought them a new one."

"Have you tried asking them to turn it down?" asked Russ.

"We did, actually. That's when they turned it up."

The call to prayer soon passed. We drank a few more beers and a few more gin-and-tonics, but we didn't get drunk. We didn't want to spoil the weekend with a hangover. We wanted to enjoy our little holiday while it lasted. By 10.30 p.m. we were back in our villa, making the most of our temporary comforts.

We returned to the pool the following morning. The transport for our next tasking – a trip to nearby Camp Blackhorse to film a training exercise with the ANA's Route Clearance Company – wasn't due to leave the Embassy until midday, giving us a few hours to live the high life in the sunshine.

I swam ten lengths of the pool, then lay out on one of the dozen vacant sun loungers. Ordinarily the idea of sunbathing in Afghanistan struck me as ridiculous, but now it made perfect sense. What else were we going to do? Stay in the villa and watch

TV? I stared up at the brilliant blue sky, allowing my skin to brown slowly in the gentle mid-morning heat, my trance only broken by the occasional helicopters – mostly Black Hawks – buzzing overhead.

The time passed by very quickly that morning. Soon we had to leave the pool and the villa and make our way over to Camp Blackhorse. Scott said goodbye to us outside the Embassy's front gate. "You owe me some Heinekens," he half-joked – and then we were gone, sucked back into the Kabul traffic in our faithful Land Cruisers.

Camp Blackhorse was off the Jalalabad Road, a few kilometres to the east of Alamo. It was home to an ANA recruit centre, birthing new units at an incredible rate. Like the training centre at Shorabak, it turned infantrymen around in eight weeks. One of the Blackhorse officers – a chubby, forthright British major called Danica – led us into the camp's prefabricated offices and gave us a comprehensive brief on the training programme.

"We are not deploying op-ready units," he said. "We do not have the time. They have 'defensive survivability'. We do our best, but if we wanted to prepare them for offensive operations, we'd need to hold them here for at least twice as long. But that ain't gonna happen, for a whole heap of reasons, mainly political."

The ambitious schedule for ANA recruitment did not lend itself to a rigorous selection process. The latest green-on-blue attack had taken place just a week earlier at a patrol base in Urozgan Province. An Australian – Lance Corporal Andrew Gordon Jones – was shot dead by an Afghan soldier who was a recent arrival at the base. He'd fled after the shooting and had not been seen since. Within hours of the murder, the Taliban had claimed him as one of their own, planted months earlier – but this was dismissed by the Australian Defence Minister Stephen Smith.

"We are aware the Taliban will use whatever propaganda they can to try and undermine the international community's efforts in Afghanistan," Smith had told Sky News. "Our starting point is that this soldier was subject to all of the usual biometric identification tests. We don't know whether there's been a dispute or disagreement between the two or what the motivation is."

Despite the apparent lack of evidence supporting the Taliban's claims, the *Guardian* published a story on "blue-on-green"* attacks the following day, quoting the Taliban spokesman (presumably Zabiullah Mujahid), but not including the comments made by Stephen Smith. It ran under the headline "Taliban Behind Surge in Attacks on Western Troops and Advisers".†

Regardless of whether the insider attacks were the result of sleeper agents or just disgruntled recruits, there were a growing number of articles in the media about the ANA's shortcomings ahead of the withdrawal of ISAF combat troops by the 2014 deadline. The *Guardian* subsequently ran an interview with a doctor called Abdul Baseer, who worked at a 100-bed military hospital in Kandahar:

> [Abdul Baseer] says he has seen clear progress in the war... but ask if he thinks the ANA is anywhere near ready to go it alone, without the help of American troops, and he lets out a panicked shout: "No! These improvements can't be sustained without their help."

The article then focused on Barack Obama's plans to cut the number of US troops in Afghanistan over the next twelve months.

---

* The correct wording is "green-on-blue", derived from the phrase "blue-on-blue", which traditionally refers to friendly-fire incidents. For Afghanistan, "blue" refers to ISAF, while "green" refers to Afghan forces.

† *The Guardian* (online), 31st May 2011.

The US President was due to make an announcement about a big reduction in numbers, meaning "a larger share of the burden… to be taken up by the ANA".

> To that end the army has been going through breakneck growth in the last 18 months, although western officials argue that the real leap in capability is yet to come as the huge influx of fresh recruits undergo more training and pick up battlefield experience.*

Major Danica wasn't about to disagree with the above sentiments: he knew all about the required leap in capability. He took us through a number of slides at Blackhorse, describing the comprehensive goals of the training programme.

"As you probably know, we're trying to get the ANA up to 195,000 before 2013,"† he said. "It's all about boots on the ground. At the very least we'll try to get units up to 85 per cent strength before deploying them. Sometimes we'll get engineer units that are just filled with infantry. It's unfortunate, but we need to keep things moving.

"When they leave here, if they're going to Helmand, they'll be taking casualties within days. That is the sad reality of the situation."

---

* *The Guardian* (online), 21st June 2011: 'Afghan Army Successes Cannot Mask Fear of What Happens when US Goes'.

† The ANA hit its target by April 2012, six months ahead of schedule.

Theatre Realities

Three British servicemen were killed in Helmand during our week in Kabul. Faulkner told us at the start of his brief on our first night back at Bastion. Corporal Michael John Pike from the Highlanders died after his patrol came under fire along Highway 601 in Pupalzay, Lance Corporal Martin Joseph Gill from 42 Commando died after his patrol came under fire in Nahr-e Saraj and Rifleman Martin Jon Lamb from 1 Rifles died after his patrol struck an IED, also in Nahr-e Saraj.

Faulkner had also started to announce the daily number of "significant acts" across theatre. These generally referred to all the deaths and serious injuries, along with the odd weapons and drugs find.

"Sixty significant acts across the whole of Afghanistan today," he told us that evening. "It was a hundred a few days ago, so it's dropped."

This was progress, apparently. The loss of the three British troops notwithstanding, the fighting season was failing to live up to its reputation. You could always find bad news in Afghanistan, but this at least was something positive.

Even Ross Kemp had failed to see any action. He'd spent three weeks with 45 Commando and the US Marines, but hadn't been shot at once. He and his team were due in at midnight, theoretically with all their kit.

"They've had some dramas with the flight programme again," Faulkner said. "They took so much kit it had to be taken off a Merlin and put on a Chinook."

I imagined Ross would've been pleased with that, but apparently it had caused all sorts of ructions with the flight planners.

"We are the dog," Faulkner said, "and these guys are the tail. They do not wag us."

Ross came into the office the following morning. His kit was spread out all over the place, a lot of it still at the flight line. He stood in the doorway and looked menacing, very much like his old character from *EastEnders*.

"We need to sort out this mess with the kit," he said.

Nobody said anything. Nobody leapt up to help.

Ross looked menacing for a moment longer and then walked out.

"What's his problem?" said Harriet. "He had to carry his own bags? Who gives a shit?"

"He needs a big hug," said Dougie. "Well, his ego needs a big hug."

I saw Ross again before lunch. He'd finally managed to get all his kit together and was drinking a coffee outside the office.

"Have we done something wrong?" he asked. "I walked in there earlier, and it was very frosty."

Sometimes he really did talk like a thespian, rather than a war reporter.

"Oh, you know what it's like," I mumbled. "Office environment. People get a bit scratchy."

Even with the kit issue sorted, Ross continued to dominate the conversation in the office. The focus now shifted onto his lack of "bang-bang" footage. He was due to return to the UK in two days, but was already making plans to return as soon as possible.

"He's a broken man," said Dougie. "He never heard so much as a shot fired."

"And the story is *progress*," Faulkner said. "It might not be what he wants, but it's the facts."

I picked up the TV remote control and switched on BFBS.* I was tired of hearing about Ross Kemp. BFBS was showing a new series called *Our War*, based on helmet-cam footage taken by British soldiers in Afghanistan. The first episode showed members of 1 Royal Anglians on patrol in Now Zad back in 2007. They passed a series of deserted buildings, all bomb-damaged and crumbling, and then came under fire.

"This isn't good," said Ali, as the soldiers screamed orders and returned fire. "Where are the key messages in this?"

"We have thought about this," said Dougie. "We're going to do a 'Then and Now' piece. In the next few days, we'll put out a story about how much Now Zad has improved."

The *Our War* footage had been cleared by the MoD back in the UK, but they now wanted the JMOC to highlight "modern-day" Now Zad. Dougie had volunteered to go over there and write an article for the British press. He was going to take some pictures of the town centre and interview a few of the locals.

Unfortunately a NATO jet had dropped a number of bombs into the centre of Now Zad only two weeks earlier, killing at least nine civilians.

"Dougie, I think talking to the locals might not be the best plan," Faulkner said. "They're still clearing the rubble."

On the plus side, the number of significant acts continued to fall. By Sunday night it was down to forty-five. A Royal Marine had been caught by an IED blast during a vehicle move in Nahr-e Saraj, but had escaped with relatively minor injuries (if a damaged airway can be considered "minor"). The base at Lashkar Gah had been on the receiving end of an attempted IDF attack, but the projectile had missed by some 600 metres.

---

* British Forces Broadcasting Service.

Ross Kemp and his team left us the following morning. He had been very quiet since his return from the field, spending a lot of time in his tent. He wasn't a "broken man", of course, but he was seriously disappointed. Progress or no progress, he wanted some "bang-bang" footage, and he hadn't got it. He was now looking to return to Helmand as soon as possible, before the fighting season was over completely. Faulkner raised the issue in his weekly report, summarizing the JMOC's tasks and priorities:

> A "heads-up" that the Tiger Aspect team (spurred by Kemp in particular) are looking for a return to theatre in July. It is clear that despite three weeks here without any noticeable kinetic incidents, Kemp is still trying to be involved in some "action" as per his previous embeds and create interest in his musings via this angle, despite the changes in Afghan life he has seen.

No sooner was Ross on his way back to the UK than things started to pick up. The US Marines took more casualties, triggering a large IED during a foot patrol in Sangin. Five of them were flown into Bastion, one without his legs. Another four US Marines were flown into Bastion – also from Sangin – after their foot patrol triggered two IEDs: one died from his wounds, the other three lost various limbs. Meanwhile – still in Sangin – a US Marine had died after insurgents had engaged his patrol with an RPG.

"Sounds like it's kicking off again," Faulkner said at the brief the following evening. "Sixty significant events across theatre today, which doesn't sound too bad, but quite a few are coming out of Sangin."

He went through the latest incidents. Three US Marines had come into Bastion with gunshot wounds following two separate engagements in Sangin. During one of the engagements, a US jet had dropped a 500-lb bomb over the insurgents' firing point, forcing them to withdraw. An Afghan child from the same area was later brought into Bastion with multiple gunshot and shrapnel wounds. The cause of the injuries was not known. An investigation had been launched.

The following day – 15th June – the hospital at Bastion went "black". That meant they were temporarily unable to take any more admissions. Eighteen casualties were brought in during a four-hour period. For several hours afterwards, casualties normally bound for Bastion had to be redirected to other ISAF hospitals across theatre.

The JMOC had more pressing concerns, however. PJHQ were upset because we'd just released a story about Ross Kemp to the *Daily Star*. His presence in Afghanistan was supposed to remain a secret from the British media for another two days. Sky was due to make a big announcement on the 17th about the third series of *Ross Kemp in Afghanistan*. Apparently PJHQ had promised them media silence until then.

The story in question involved a young soldier who had just arrived at Bastion. Back in the UK, he'd designed a T-shirt bearing the legend "I Joined the Army to Meet Ross Kemp". It was in his kit bag, along with the rest of his uniform. Having discovered that Ross was in the neighbourhood, he wandered over to the JMOC with his T-shirt and asked for a picture with the big man. Ross was only too happy to oblige, posing alongside the young soldier and his T-shirt. Ali had taken the picture, and Dougie had sent it to the *Daily Star*.

"We're getting bollocked for releasing a shot of Ross Kemp," Dougie said. "It's ridiculous."

We were sitting in the late-afternoon sunshine, drinking coffee. Mick had joined us, shaking his head as he stepped out of the office.

"A Chinook has just flown in with another load of multiple amputees," he said. "And they're worried about a picture of Ross Kemp. They've got no sense of perspective."

"Exactly," Dougie said. "Think about all the guys who've had limbs blown off. If you put them in a group photo, you'd be shocked. PJHQ wouldn't want you to see that."

I thought about the numerous amputees I'd seen at Chetwynd Barracks in Chilwell during my mobilization training. The soldier in the stores, issuing our kit, was missing an arm. The soldier in the headquarters, sorting out all our pay and paperwork, was missing an arm. The ex-Gunner in the suit, giving us a presentation on the importance of insurance, was missing an arm. For all I knew, they could've been missing their legs as well, their injuries hidden by their trousers.

"Someone needs to report all these injuries," Mick said.

I pondered his words. Lieutenant Colonel Mike McErlain had already had a go, sending his hospital diary to the *Sunday Mirror* – but was that enough? Should it be left at that? Was it the final word on the alarming normality of traumatic amputations at Bastion? Or should the reporting continue as long as the war continued?

I left Dougie and Mick and went to Heroes for some time to myself. It was my birthday, but I hadn't told anybody. It didn't feel right bringing it up. Just a few hundred yards away, the hospital was full to bursting point, many of the beds taken by fresh amputees. It was not a day for celebrating.

I bought a coffee – my fifth of the day – and sat in the corner at one of the tables farthest from the television. *Jackass* was showing on BFBS, the volume turned right up. I took my birthday cards out of my trouser-leg pocket, reading through the messages again. Four of them had arrived that morning, right on time, my family and friends not letting me down. Normally I read my mail in private, but that afternoon it didn't matter. My fellow coffee drinkers – US Marines, mostly – were too busy watching the movie, laughing at the pratfalls, to notice a sentimental British captain in the corner.

My parents had sent me a card with a picture of a springer spaniel on the front, feigning indifference to a tennis ball right in front of his nose. Inside my mother had written:

Liebster Christian,

For your birthday I wish you everything you dream of and loads of health and happiness too. We are looking forward so much to have you home again soon. The dogs will go mad! I don't know if this card will arrive in time, but we will be thinking of you every minute of the day (we do that anyway!). And I must not tell you that we will have a bottle of bubbly – that would not be fair!

    All my love as always, stay safe,

                    Your Mum xxxxx

Beneath my mother's words, my father had also written a message, his sentiments a little more concise:

We are missing you loads here, especially the dogs. Keep your powder dry and don't let the buggers get you down.

I smiled at my father's brevity, then put the cards away. On the television, *Jackass* was coming to an end. For the final scene, the cast had filmed themselves being "blown up" in slow motion, standing in the centre of a lounge rigged with small amounts of carefully placed explosives. Bits of vase, bookcase and piano flew towards the camera, all of the cast gurning for comic effect as the shock wave engulfed them.

Nobody in Heroes was laughing. We all watched the explosion in stony-faced silence, trying to imagine what it would really be like, caught inside the radius of an actual bomb blast.

Maybe some of the Marines already knew.

I went back to the JMOC, thinking about the hospital again, thinking about what Mick had said. Who exactly was going to report all these injuries? The embeds who came through the JMOC got up close and personal with the troops all the time, and they bore witness to their suffering, but it was war reporting on a controlled scale, a microscale. They lived with a unit for a week, they wrote their story, and then they went home. It was fine as far as it went, but it was a very tight focus. There was no sense of relativity. How often was this kind of stuff happening? Were these injuries normal? What was "normal" anyway?

I was due to catch a late flight to Lashkar Gah for a short task, but that wasn't for another five hours. I still had plenty of time to loiter in the office, in and around the vicinity of the Ops Watch laptop, checking all the hospital admissions for that day:

05.46 Nad-e Ali
45 Commando, Non-Battle Injury: 1 x Cat B*
1st/2nd degree petrol burn 6% of right leg, 2% of left leg

06.37 Nahr-e Saraj
Scots Dragoon Guards, Non-Battle Injury: 1 x Cat A
Chest pains

---

*   Injuries were graded A to C according to severity. Medical Emergency Response Teams aimed to get Cat A classifications – such as traumatic amputees – into hospital within a maximum of ninety minutes, although the vast majority arrived inside the "golden hour". Cat B injuries needed hospital treatment within four hours, while Cat C injuries could wait up to twenty-four hours.

08.14 Nahr-e Saraj
British Non-Battle Injury: 1 x Cat B
Appendicitis

09.06 Nahr-e Saraj
Scots Dragoon Guards, Non-Battle Injury: 1 x Cat C
Recurring achilles injury/infected tendon

11.31 Nahr-e Saraj
US Marines, dismounted patrol IED strike: 1 x Cat A
Both legs – below knee amp

11.33 Nahr-e Saraj
ISAF civilian, Non-Battle Injury: 1 x Cat A
Dehydration

11.58 Nahr-e Saraj
Afghan civilian: 1 x Cat A
2 x gunshot wounds to chest, gunshot wound to left arm
(ISAF not involved)

12.03 Musa Qalah
Afghan civilian vehicle IED strike: 1 x Cat A, 1 x Cat B
Skull fracture, soft tissue injuries to face, right tib/fib open
Bilateral lower ext fracture

12.43 Lashkar Gah
British Non-Battle Injury: 1 x Cat B
Torsion, left testicle

12.52 Nahr-e Saraj
US Marines, IED strike: 1 x Cat A
Shrapnel right knee, bleeding

13.49 Sangin
US Marines, dismounted patrol IED strike: 3 x Cat A, 4 x Cat B
Triple amp – both legs, right hand
Shrapnel to face – bleeding
Shrapnel to face – bleeding
Triple amp – bleeding
Shrapnel to face – bleeding
Shrapnel to face – bleeding
Left perforated eardrum, lacerations to the left side of face, possible jaw fracture

15.18 Nahr-e Saraj
C Sqn, Scots Dragoon Guards: 2 x Cat B
Heat Injury x 2

15.23 Nahr-e Saraj South
Afghan civilian males: 2 x Cat A
Gunshot wound to left shoulder
IED – frag injuries to right leg and right arm

17.09 Nad-e Ali
42 Commando, Non-Battle Injury: 1 x Cat C
Severe ankle sprain

17.29 Nahr-e Saraj
S Coy, 1 Rifles: 1 x Cat A
Heat injury and spasms

18.17 Lashkar Gah
B Coy, 4 Scots, Non-Battle Injury: 1 x Cat C
Dislocated patella

19.06 Kajaki,
US Marines, 1 x Cat A
Heat injury

19.55 Nad-e Ali
M Coy, 42 Commando, Non-Battle Injury: 1 x Cat C
Infected red eye

At least the British injuries seemed fairly innocuous – just some heat casualties and a few knocks and sprains. It was the Americans who had taken the real hits, suffering another God-awful afternoon in Sangin.

For the sake of balance, I had a look at the "credit" column as well. It was always good to know the insurgents weren't having much fun either:

10.05 Musa Qala
US Marines positively identified 4 insurgents establishing a firing position. Confirmed no civilians in area, then fired 2 Excal rounds (155-mm artillery) onto target, which impacted with good effect. Friendly forces then observed 2 more insurgents approaching the strike site with Soviet-style weapons. Friendly forces called repeat and fired another 2 rounds, which also impacted with good effect. 5 insurgents killed in action (unconfirmed).

19.57 Now Zad
British Apache positively identified 6 x insurgents hiding in a wadi. The wadi is the known location of a weapons cache and

the individuals were also exhibiting hostile intent. Apache fired 133 x 30 mm, resulting in 4 insurgents killed in action.

20.30 Nahr-e Saraj
Dragoons Mechanized Infantry Company received small-arms fire from insurgents. Returned fire with small arms and heavy machine gun. No friendly casualties at this stage. The enemy has ceased firing. Believed to be a total of 6 insurgents killed in action.

* * *

The following day was much worse for British troops. A total of nineteen casualties were flown into Bastion, including one fatality. I was able to check Ops Watch in the TFH office at Lashkar Gah that evening. Russ and I had spent the day walking around the base with the camera and tripod, asking bemused soldiers to record messages for Armed Forces Day.* It had been a boring, frustrating process – some of them needed up to ten takes just to smile at the camera and say "Many thanks for all your support on Armed Forces Day, from all of us here in Helmand Province" – but at least it was all for a good cause, highlighting the efforts (and the sacrifices) of the troops in Afghanistan.

05.57 Nahr-e Saraj
IED strike: 3 x US Cat B
Lacerations to face
Lacerations to face
Hearing loss

---

*   An annual event in the UK, raising awareness of British forces and giving the public a chance to show their support.

06.36 Nahr-e Saraj
A Coy, 1 Rifles, dismounted patrol: IED strike
2 x GBR Cat A, 2 x GBR Cat B, 1 x GBR Cat C, 1 x Afghan
interpreter Cat C
GBR: frag to lower leg, neck and face
GBR: frag to upper and lower leg
TERP: frag to knee and lower leg
GBR: frag to leg and hip, bleeding heavily, slipping in and out
of consciousness, possible broken femur
GBR: frag to shoulder
GBR: frag to lower leg

07.05 Nad Ali
Estonian mounted patrol, IED strike: 1 x Cat A. At 08:20, an
insurgent threw a grenade at the patrol: 1 x Cat B.
IED casualty: Contusion, fractured right ankle, suspected inter-
nal bleeding
Grenade casualty: frag to upper left thigh, lower left leg and
head – a lot of swelling in frag area

08.58: Nahr-e Saraj
A Coy, 2 Royal Gurkha Rifles dismounted patrol, IED strike:
1 x GBR Cat A
Shrapnel to right-hand side of body – conscious, bleeding heav-
ily, severe pain

09.57 Sangin
US Marines Non-Battle Injury: 1 x Cat B (hydraulic pressure on
GPR panels gave out, panels fell and crushed arm).
Broken arm and lacerations, swelling and light bleeding

12.42 Lashkar Gah
1 x GBR Cat C non-battle injury
Chronic bilateral knee pain

15.43 Nahr-e Saraj
Task Force Helmand Warthog Group, IED strike:
1 x GBR Cat A, 1 x GBR Cat B
Cat A: chest and side trauma
Cat B: possible fracture to right forearm

16.57 Nahr-e Saraj
Task Force Helmand Warthog Group, 2 x IED strikes:
1 x GBR killed in action, 1 x GBR Cat A and 1 x GBR Cat B
A mounted patrol was conducting security operations 500 m north of Highway 1 when a Warthog struck an IED. The strike resulted in 1 x Cat A and 1 x Cat B. At 17:30, reports of multiple IEDs in the area of strike – could be a possible minefield. Another Warthog strikes a second IED, resulting in death. At 19:48, friendly forces discover another 2 possible IEDs. Later detonated – both had 20 kg main charges.
1st IED: No details on Cat A and Cat B
2nd IED: Lower body amputation – casualty died of wounds. Declared dead by ground call sign.

Death or Glory

On the evening of 17th June we returned to the base on the outskirts of Gereshk, the scene of our previous stay with the Household Cavalry. It was now home to the 9th/12th Royal Lancers, our hosts for the next twenty-four hours. Russ and I would be shooting patrol footage and interviews for BBC *East Midlands Today*, broadcasting in the heart of the Lancers' recruiting patch, while Ali was planning to target some of the local newspapers – *Leicester Mercury*, *Nottingham Evening Post* – with photographs and home-town stories.

I slept badly that night. We were staying with ten other soldiers in a narrow room under a ceiling thick with cobwebs. An electric fan stood to the side of each camp cot, whirring in the darkness. It was cooler than I had any right to expect, but it was still too hot. I lay awake for hours, naked inside the faux privacy of my mosquito net, sweating about all the usual stuff that goes through your mind the night before a deployment. At one point, just to add to the psychodrama, a cockroach scuttled across my chest. I ignored it, but then, two minutes later, it crawled across my face. Now it felt like I was in a fucking crypt. I switched on my torch and found the shiny little monster underneath my camp cot, sitting on my trousers. I couldn't be bothered to kill him – he had nothing to do with this war, and I couldn't face the crunching sound – so I put a mug over him and went back to "sleep".

The pitiful bleeping alarm on my digital watch went off at 6 a.m. Soldiers stirred in the half-light. Fortunately, I'd managed to get a few hours' sleep. I got dressed and took my little friend – he seemed happy enough, nestled inside the mug – out into the vehicle yard, depositing him as far away from the living area as possible. He scurried across the gravel, disappearing into some weeds that were growing up against the perimeter wall.

Maybe I should've killed him, but that would've felt like bad luck. I had less than four weeks to push until my flight home, and I wasn't about to start tempting fate. Omens were looming up everywhere, and they were impossible to ignore. I walked back into the living area, where the camp dog – a friendly, underweight golden retriever – nuzzled my leg, looking for a pat on the head. I duly obliged, accidentally treading on his tail in the process. He yelped out in pain, triggering an explosion of bad karma. I felt terrible. No matter that he was OK, quickly seeking out my hand for another pat on the head: the damage was done.

We rolled out of camp after breakfast. I was in the lead vehicle, which didn't bode well, but at least it was a Husky. Russ and Ali were in the Jackal behind me, getting all their shots and footage of life on Highway 1. We drove for twenty minutes before dismounting on the forecourt of a disused petrol station. Three soldiers stayed with the vehicles while the rest of us spread out in single file and patrolled out into the desert, making our way over to a small compound on a ridge overlooking the highway. It was home to one of the local elders, a bearded man in a white robe who came out to meet us. He chatted to the patrol commander for ten minutes, telling him his woes.

"This country has been destroyed," he said. "There is nothing here."

"If you keep talking to us, we can help you," said the patrol commander. "If we know who the insurgents are, we can stop them. We can help rebuild this country."

We continued into the desert, performing a large loop through a series of compounds. Children stood in doorways, watching us with the eyes of old men. We gave them boiled sweets, and they became youngsters again, smiling for our cameras, asking for *chockalit*.

We got back to the vehicles at midday and returned to base for some lunch, weaving through the traffic on Highway 1. This was the beauty of the cavalry ethos – have wagon, will travel. By 12.45 p.m. we were back in the cookhouse, eating chicken pasta and drinking orange squash.

After lunch I interviewed some of the soldiers in the shadeless vehicle yard. It was roasting hot now – around 43°C – but Russ needed to frame his shots with a decent backdrop. Each of the soldiers took their turn standing in front of a Jackal, telling me all about themselves and their work in Afghanistan.

"I'm from Loughborough," said the first one, a young trooper called Toby.

"Really?" I said. "I used to go to school in Loughborough."

He stared at me for a moment. "Actually, I'm from Essex. I just live in Loughborough."

"That's fine," I said. "What do you miss about Loughborough?"

"Uni chicks," he said. "And getting tanked up."

"OK," I said. "We'll probably leave that out."

"No worries."

"So what do you do out here?"

"I've got two jobs," he said. "I drive the Jackal for the boss, and I'm the point man on the patrols."

"What's that like?"

"It's scary being the point man, because obviously you're the first man into contact, but it's also quite rewarding. It's been hairy at times, but that's what you expect. That's what you join the army for."

All the soldiers I interviewed said they were glad to be out here. Some of them even spoke with relish about the opportunities for combat.

"The tour's been really good," said Sam, a lance corporal from Nottinghamshire. "It's been lairy in some places, and quiet in other places. It's the same with every tour."

"What's been the best part of the tour?"

"I like the contacts," he said. "I like going out, looking for the Taliban. It gets the adrenaline going. And when you get into a fight with them, you feel great afterwards."

After the interviews, we went out again. I felt much less superstitious than I had done before: the fear of bad omens had worn off. Interviewing the soldiers had been a strangely calming experience, despite all their ramblings about combat. It brought a degree of comfort knowing a little bit more about the men alongside you. So often the Combat Camera Team was just an attachment, stuck onto the side of a patrol for a limited amount of time. Talking to the soldiers at least created a greater sense of belonging, which brought with it a greater sense of security.

We drove in the same formation as before, heading along Highway 1 to another checkpoint. The plan was to interview one of the local ANA commanders, getting some all-important "Afghan face" for the East Midlands piece. After that – somewhat randomly – we were going to film a few of our guys eating rations for *The One Show*. The BBC producers were lining up an interview with the Ministry of Defence gastronome responsible for producing all the different menus in our ration boxes, and they wanted us to provide some footage of British soldiers tucking into their boil-in-the-bag food while out on the Afghan front line.

It was only a fifteen-minute drive to the checkpoint, but halfway there we were brought to a halt by two Jackals parked across the road. They were part of a security cordon for an IED that had just been discovered by the roadside about a hundred metres up ahead. A team from the Royal Engineers was preparing to blow the device up and get the road open again.

We wanted to film it, obviously. It was going to be a loud explosion. We had no footage of IED blasts on this tour, so it was something we felt we needed to capture. We gave no thought to the fact that this barbarous little device – undiscovered – would've blown us off the road. We just set up our video camera on a tripod and happily waited for the Royal Engineers to give us our money shot.

We didn't have to wait long. A lone engineer crouched over the device for a moment, before retreating back to the safety of his vehicle. We got a thirty-second warning over the radio, then the IED detonated with a ground-shaking bang, throwing up a mushroom cloud of smoke and dust thirty feet into the air. Russ watched the whole thing through his video camera, recording on his tripod, while Ali took her shots leaning against one of the Jackals for support. I captured the moment for posterity as well, taking a couple of hurried shots on my crappy Fuji camera. It had a dodgy lens and a slow shutter speed – it was probably worth about a thirtieth of Ali's Nikon D3S – but it did at least come with some sentimental value, being a leaving gift from some of my nicer colleagues at Smooth Radio.

By now the ANA commander had turned up on the scene, so we hurried through an interview with him, still standing in the middle of Highway 1 as the Royal Engineers packed up in the background. He'd seen it all before, and was more than a little jaded with the constant struggle to keep the roadside clear of IEDs. He had the same haunted brown eyes that you found on all Afghan men over the age of forty, and they obviously coloured his view of the war.

"What it's like working with the British forces?" I asked him.

"It is good; you are good," he said. "But when you go, then what happens?"

He stared at me for a long moment, as though he actually expected me to give him an answer. I didn't have one for him, of course, so all I could do was pretend he was being rhetorical and move on to the next question.

Most of the interview was unusable (he wasn't a great one for key messaging), but I knew the footage of the IED going up would guarantee the piece some decent airtime. There was precious little Afghan face, but at least we could show that the Lancers and the Royal Engineers were finding IEDs and destroying them, making the road safe, keeping it open for business. There was a slight risk of negative messaging, given that they'd found an IED at all, but I could live with that.

With the sun beginning to set, we had just enough time to film the rations sequence for *The One Show*. We drove a little way out into the desert and parked up the vehicles in a hollow square. One of the younger guys got some water on the boil, heating up a selection of our meals, while the rest of us sat on the ground against the sides of the vehicles and chatted. We talked about all kinds of rubbish, all of it good-humoured banter, all of it a million miles away from the countless horrors that could befall any one of us in this country. None of us mentioned the fact that, had we been driving down Highway 1 about an hour earlier, we could now have been stuck inside Bastion hospital instead, either getting the trauma-bay treatment or waiting and praying in the corridor. Instead we just poked fun at each other and watched the sun sink into the horizon.

After ten minutes, the rations were ready. We had chicken-and-mushroom pasta, spaghetti bolognese and lamb curry. I moved from soldier to soldier, trying to get their opinions on the various dishes as Russ filmed, but it was hopeless. To a man, they all took the piss out of the food, spooning it into their mouths and making over-the-top groaning noises to signal their appreciation.

"Seriously guys, just give me something I can use."

Only the squadron commander, a very well-spoken major known as Docs who had tagged along with the patrol, took the filming even vaguely seriously. I came to him last.

"This tastes absolutely delicious," he said, raising a spoonful of bolognese to his lips. "It really hits the spot."

He was probably taking the piss as well, but he had such a posh voice he could get away with it.

We returned to Bastion later that evening, the Lancers offering us a lift in a small convoy of Huskies and Jackals that happened to be going that way. It took about two hours to get there, but it was better than hanging around for another twenty-four hours waiting for our scheduled flight. A long vehicle move at night was riskier than a short trip in a helicopter, but it meant we would have an extra day for editing (i.e. a day off), so we opted for the road.

"There's no point worrying about getting hit, boss," said Russ. "If it's going to happen, it's going to happen. There's nothing you can do about it."

I wasn't entirely convinced by Russ's logic, but I agreed to the change of plan anyway. Personally, I thought it was easier to go with the belief that bad things only ever happened to other people. It was now a favourite coping strategy of mine, a touch on the dubious side, but usable nonetheless. You had to think that way most days, otherwise you'd lose your nerve completely.

Cameraman Down

The following day – Sunday 19th June – was indeed a very easy day. We did do some editing, but we also went to the gym, drank a lot of coffee and sorted out some personal admin. Sundays were always quiet in the JMOC, and by mid-afternoon the office was usually empty, save for any volunteer willing to stay inside and man the phones. On this occasion, it was me, so I took a seat and went through the latest incidents on Ops Watch. Op Minimize had been called that morning, so I started with the Helmand feed.

In Nahr-e Saraj, at 09.48, Royal Marines from 42 Commando had come under small-arms fire from insurgents at Checkpoint Sorab. They were unable to identify the insurgents' position and did not return fire. One Marine had suffered a gunshot wound and was transported to Patrol Base 5, then flown to Bastion in forty-seven minutes.

At 11.40 in Kajaki, 3 km south-west of FOB Zeebrugge, a foot patrol from 2nd Battalion 12th US Marines had struck an IED containing around 40 lbs of home-made explosive. One of the soldiers lost both his legs in the blast. He was flown to the medical facility at FOB Edi, but died of his wounds. Another IED – containing 10 lbs of home-made explosive – was later found in the same area, but safely detonated.

Later, at 15.02, in Nahr-e Saraj, 2 km south-west of Salaang, a foot patrol from 1 Rifles had struck an IED in an irrigation ditch.

Two of the soldiers had shrapnel wounds to the neck; one took shrapnel to the leg and one had a possible dislocated shoulder. Their Afghan interpreter took shrapnel to the arm. All of them had been flown back to Bastion in thirty-two minutes.

After the Helmand feed, I looked through the most significant acts across the rest of the country. It was the usual list of brutal calamities involving ISAF and Afghan forces, although a couple of incidents with civilians had also been flagged up. In Kunduz a mounted patrol carrying a Provincial Reconstruction Team had been hit by a car bomb. Two Afghan civilians had been killed and eleven were injured. Two German soldiers received minor injuries and were able to return to duty. The PRT Commander was not in the damaged vehicle and was able to reach his meeting as planned.

Meanwhile in Kandahar, a combined mounted patrol from 3rd Afghan Border Police (ABP) Zone and 1st Squadron 38th US Cavalry Regiment was involved in a collision with an Afghan civilian vehicle in the Spin Boldak District. One of the vehicles in the convoy – complete with mine roller – struck the Afghan vehicle, seriously injuring four civilians, including two children. Three other civilians were also injured. They were flown to the hospital at Kandahar. An investigation had been launched.

I sat in the office, making a note of these incidents, because I felt that someone should. It felt like the right thing to do. The war wasn't just about statistics – it wasn't just about a graph that showed "significant acts" going up or down. You had to have the details – you had to put some flesh on the figures – otherwise you just had numbers on a page.

The office filled up again for the brief that evening. Faulkner gave us all his usual comments and updates, along with some of the latest figures churned out by the Intelligence cell.

"There were 342 IED events across the whole of Afghanistan over the last month," he said. "And 846 security incidents. That's about the same as previous months and years."

It was all just carnage, the entire country. I went to bed feeling depressed. I couldn't see how on earth this place was ever going to turn itself around.

I fell asleep reading *Chickenhawk*. I was near the end now and, strangely, I found it quite relaxing. The Vietnam described by the author was truly ravaged and hopeless. But if that country could drag itself out of such horrors, then maybe there was some hope for Afghanistan.

I was woken up by the voice of Russ. It was 11.45 p.m. His head was poking around the side of the camouflage sheet that was effectively my bedroom door.

"Boss."

"Hi, Russ." I sat up, feeling a little self-conscious. "What's up?"

"I've just spoken to my wife. We've got a medical emergency at home. She's been in touch with the compassionate cell in the UK, and I could be going back."

"Is your wife OK?"

"She is, she's OK," he said. "She's just speaking to the compassionate cell now."

It transpired that a close relative of Russ's wife had fallen seriously ill. A nurse from the compassionate cell was going to speak to the doctors in the morning. Following her take on the situation, we'd know what was happening with Russ.

The following day was spent pretty much in limbo, as we waited to hear back from the UK. Russ didn't know whether he'd be staying in Afghanistan or going back to the UK for good. There wasn't a great deal he could do other than stay in touch with his wife and pack some of his kit.

We got the phone call in the evening. It had been decreed that Russ was a "Compassionate B". That meant two weeks' leave back in the UK, with immediate effect.

The next Tristar was leaving within the hour. Having spent the day in a fog of uncertainty, Russ was suddenly in a rush. He had about twenty minutes to get the rest of his kit together and get over to the flight line. There was virtually no time for proper goodbyes. He gave everyone in the JMOC a quick round of handshakes, then Ali gave him a big hug.

"Take care of yourself," she said, as though she was never going to see him again.

"He'll be back in two weeks, Ali," I said, although her reaction did give me pause for thought. Compassionate cases were a moveable feast, and once a soldier was back in the UK, any number of circumstances could change.

"Have a safe journey," I said to Russ finally, shaking his hand. "I'll see you soon."

"See you, boss," he said, a big grin on his face.

And then he picked up his bags, climbed into the minibus with Mick behind the wheel, and was gone.

Wear Your Uniform to Work

Russ's departure meant our shooting schedule for the next two weeks had to be thrown out. Without a cameraman I was something of a spare part. Ali at least was able to perform a few localized jobs, photographing VIP visits by the likes of the Defence Secretary Liam Fox, but there was little for me to do short of cutting audio from previous interviews and pushing it out to radio stations back in the UK.

This meant spending a lot of time in the JMOC, editing on my laptop. Which in turn meant spending some quality time with Faulkner, Dougie and Harriet. Once again I had the opportunity to see the minutiae of their daily office grind at first hand. It was not a pretty sight.

The day after Russ's departure – 22nd June – was "Wear Your Uniform to Work Day" back in the UK. It was an annual initiative designed to promote the reserve forces to employers. It wasn't compulsory for reservists to participate, but it was encouraged. The MoD always ran a big publicity campaign – tied in with Armed Forces Day – to make sure everyone knew about it.

As part of that publicity campaign, representatives from all three services were interviewed on *BBC Breakfast*, sitting on the famous red couch alongside the nation's favourites Bill Turnbull and Sian Williams. The television in the JMOC was always turned to *BBC Breakfast* in the morning, supposedly to provide some light relief from the usual slurry of rolling news.

First up was a spokeswoman from the RAF. She looked presentable enough to me, sitting on the red couch in her dark-blue uniform, but others disagreed.

"The first thing you need to do is get a haircut," Faulkner said. "Look at that fringe."

"You can barely see her eyes," Harriet said.

"She's not even supposed to be wearing those badges on her lapels." Faulkner shook his head. He was trying to get on with his work, but the lure of imperfect military representatives on the television was too great. "She just looks wrong."

Next up came the army, represented by a female colonel with blond hair. She took to the couch in her standard camouflage combats.

"Another haircut," Faulkner said. "Unbelievable."

"It's too long," confirmed Harriet.

The colonel's hair was a little unruly, but it was barely touching her collar.

"She's got no badges on her arm," Faulkner said.

I tried to make out what the colonel was actually saying, but it was difficult, given the running commentary alongside me.

"What's with these answers?" Faulkner said. "They should be twenty- to thirty-second soundbites."

I gave up and went outside for a coffee. It was another improbably hot day, the highs now reaching 44°C. Ali was standing over by the journalists' tent, carrying out some routine checks on her kit before going to cover another VIP visit. The Foreign Secretary William Hague was in town.

"All sorted?"

"Yes, boss."

"Another day, another picture in a national newspaper."

Ali smiled and headed off. She wasn't even supposed to cover VIP visits – it was considered an inappropriate use of resources sending a Combat Camera Team photographer to cover a meet-and-greet – but she was available, and it got her away from the JMOC. She found the office even more stultifying than I did.

She would soon be back, however, to cover the sunset vigil. It was a weekly event at Bastion, held every Wednesday at 5.30 p.m. Every British serviceman and woman on camp was expected to attend, unless on duty. Hundreds of us would gather on the makeshift desert square just a short walk from the JMOC. We'd form long ranks, dozens deep, and listen to the prayers and eulogies offered up by the chaplain and the colleagues of the fallen. Ali would take photographs of the service, which were sent to the bereaved families.

If no one had died during the previous seven days, then obviously there was no vigil, but this week three soldiers had been killed in action. Six days earlier, Craftsman Andrew Found from the REME was trying to recover a damaged Warthog during an operation to detain an insurgent in Nahr-e Saraj when he was fatally wounded by an IED. On the same day, Corporal Lloyd Newell, originally of the Parachute Regiment, was killed by small-arms fire during a firefight. The third fatality – Private Gareth Bellingham from 3 Mercian – was shot dead while on patrol in Nahr-e Saraj two days later.

Only the deaths of Craftsman Found and Private Bellingham were marked at that evening's vigil. Corporal Newell was not mentioned, on account of the fact that he was actually a serving member of the SAS. Even at Bastion, the Special Forces liked to take every precaution to ensure their identities remained a secret. Their desire for anonymity was reflected in the MoD's statement on Corporal Newell's death, which listed his unit as the Parachute

Regiment (it described him as "the personification of a great British paratrooper"). It added that no details about his age or where he was from would be released "because of the nature of his work".

The MoD maintained this line in the days that followed, despite the fact that Corporal Newell's membership of the SAS had been widely reported in the British press, most prominently by Virginia Wheeler in the *Sun*.

The vigil was always followed in the early hours of the morning by the "ramp ceremony", attended by members of the losing units. This was the start of the repatriation process, whereby colleagues of the deceased loaded the coffins into the back of a Hercules. Ali took the pictures, which again went to the family.

In the case of this particular ramp ceremony, which took place as usual at around 3.30 a.m., Ali only took pictures of the coffins of Craftsman Found and Private Bellingham.

"The SAS guys came an hour earlier than everyone else," she told me the next day. "Lloyd Newell's coffin was already on the plane when I got there. They'd screened it behind a black curtain."

Once Special Forces, always Special Forces, as the saying goes.

* * *

At around the same time that Craftsman Found and Private Bellingham were being carried onto the Hercules, Barack Obama was giving a speech in the White House, televised live across the world, announcing plans to withdraw a third of US troops from Afghanistan over the next twelve months.

Many media commentators in the US were quick to point out that the bulk of the withdrawal was timed just ahead of the presidential election on 6th November 2012. It was also noted that there were just 32,000 US troops in Afghanistan on 20th January 2009, the day that President Obama took office, compared to the current total of 100,000.

The following morning, the French President Nicolas Sarkozy announced that he would also start withdrawing some of his 4,000 troops from Afghanistan. I looked through the statement he gave to the press as I sat at my desk in the JMOC, trying to look busy:

> Given the progress we have seen, France will begin a gradual withdrawal of reinforcement troops sent to Afghanistan, in a proportional manner and in a calendar comparable to the withdrawal of American reinforcements.

The statement didn't give any precise details, apparently because the French wanted to avoid giving sensitive information to the Taliban. But the French Defence Minister Gérard Longuet went on to tell France Info Radio: "It will be significant for 2012 and, like the Americans, we will see this materialize in 2012."

I moved on to other stuff. I had a trip to Kabul to organize. Russ and I had always intended to return to the ANP's Staff College to complete our filming of the five-week District Commander's course. The original plan had been to go back and record the officers graduating on their final day. It wasn't necessarily going to make for the most stellar footage, but it was going to provide us with a nice little conclusion to the piece.

With Russ flying back to the UK, I had assumed the whole thing would fall through, but now I was starting to think that maybe I could just go to Kabul on my own and do the filming myself. Ali had already been tasked to cover the Female Engagement Team*

---

* Tradition dictated that male soldiers were not to communicate directly with Afghan women, so Female Engagement Teams, or FETs, offered support in their place, building up relationships with the local females.

in Lashkar Gah (my presence – as a man – was neither required nor wanted), so her schedule was taken care of. What else was I going to do other than fester in the JMOC?

Granted, I'd never actually used the P2 video camera, but how hard could it be? You just had to point it in the right direction and press the little red record button. I wasn't making *Lawrence of Arabia*.

My flight to Kabul wasn't until Monday, which meant a long weekend stranded in the JMOC, listening to my colleagues chafe over their daily dramas. On Friday, the vital concern involved a reporter and cameraman from BBC Kabul, who had flown in on the same Hercules as another embed, *Sunday Times* correspondent Miles Amoore. Upon their arrival at the flight line, the BBC pair had accepted a lift to the JMOC from some passing American soldiers, while Miles had waited for Mick to pick him up in the minibus, as arranged.

"I'm not happy with that," said Mick when he finally got back to the JMOC with Miles. "I was supposed to be picking the BBC guys up as well. They didn't tell us they'd got a lift. We could've been waiting for ages."

"Typical BBC attitude," Faulkner said. "Get used to it."

I sunk a little lower in my seat. Faulkner had apparently forgotten that I was a BBC journalist as well, and given his antipathy towards my fellow workers, I decided it would be easier if I just remained under the radar. I had three more days in the office until my trip to Kabul, and I wasn't about to make it any harder for myself by siding with the enemy.

The BBC pair came into the office later that afternoon and seemed like perfectly nice guys. They chatted to Dougie about their schedule for the coming week, out on the ground with 4 Scots. Faulkner mumbled a few words of greeting, then continued with his work, writing reports and firing off emails. No mention was made of the "incident".

Meanwhile, Miles Amoore was keeping a low profile. I caught a glimpse of him ducking into the journalists' tent with a coffee, moving like a man who knew his way around the place. Although he wore a beard – presumably to look older – he was still only in his late twenties and had passed through the JMOC many times before. He'd been standing in more or less the same spot back in July 2009 when the news was relayed to him that his brother Jim – a second lieutenant in the Rifles – had been badly injured by an IED on the outskirts of Sangin. Miles had rushed over to the hospital, where his brother was being treated for blast wounds and shrapnel to his face, neck, arms and legs. He joined him on the flight back to the UK and spent days at his bedside in Birmingham's Selly Oak Hospital. The subsequent feature that he wrote on the experience – 'Blood Brothers Scarred by War' – won him that year's Foreign Press Association's Print/Web Feature Story of the Year Award.

Miles didn't stick around for very long. By the time I wandered back into the office the following morning, he was already gone, bound for Patrol Base 2 to do a piece with 1 Rifles.

I sat at my desk and deleted a few emails on my laptop, wondering what to do with my day. In such circumstances, I sometimes looked to my colleagues in the office for entertainment. They didn't say very much, staring fixedly at their computer screens, but when they did say something it was always noteworthy.

"He actually writes quite well," murmured Dougie. He was reading through an article by one of the embeds, making sure there was no information that would breach operational security. "But as a personality, he leaves a lot to be desired."

"Like a lot of journalists," Faulkner said. I didn't know who Dougie was referring to, but I did know that one reporter who'd already put Faulkner's back up was the *Daily Telegraph*'s Thomas Harding, who'd upset a number of senior officers by wearing British Army uniform during his embed with the Paras back in March. By all accounts, Harding felt it made him less of a target outside the wire. According to his theory, reporters dressed in conventional blue were more likely to be seen and shot by the Taliban, who would value the publicity that would come with a dead reporter.

The issue was discussed at the highest levels, with Faulkner eventually producing a report on the exact protocol regarding journalists in uniform.

"The Paras had a lack of understanding that they needed to keep him at arm's length and that he wasn't supposed to be a chum," Faulkner had said to Dougie after Harding had completed his embed. "He just kept pulling strings. Eventually he got full MTP* and helmet and body armour. The only thing he didn't have was a rifle. I don't know if he was carrying a rifle, but I fucking hope not."

Faulkner's report drew upon a number of sources, starting with the *Green Book*, which detailed MoD working arrangements with the media. It stated that there was "no specific obligation on the part of UK forces to protect individuals or installations over and above the rights of all civilians working in conflict zones set out in the Geneva Conventions and their additional protocols. Furthermore, the MoD recognizes its obligations as a UN signatory to respect the professional independence and rights of journalists, media professionals and associated personnel as civilians."

---

* Multi-Terrain Pattern – the army's new uniform, replacing the traditional green camouflage of DPM (Disruptive Pattern Material).

With regard to dress and equipment, the *Green Book* offered this:

> Accredited correspondents embedded with UK forces will be expected to equip themselves with their own personal protective equipment (e.g. body armour, helmet as advised by MoD). Correspondents will wear appropriate civilian clothing as specified by PJHQ instructions, non-military-patterned and neutral in any colour (including body armour and helmet covers), that ensures and maintains their status as non-combatants.
>
> On occasion, they may be issued with specialist protective clothing (along with any required training in its use) should the environment or situation demand. When accredited as War Correspondents they will be fully clothed and equipped with standard issue military items, and distinguished from combatants by means of distinctive media shoulder titles/armbands.

Confusingly, the Green Book talked about "war correspondents" rather than "embedded journalists". In order to clear up the distinction, Faulkner had quoted directly from an interview conducted by the International Committee of the Red Cross with one of their legal experts, Robin Geiss:

> "Embedded journalists" is a modern term. It was apparently first used during the 2003 invasion of Iraq and has since gained widespread currency. It does not occur in any provision of international humanitarian law and, so far as I know, it is not clearly defined. However, it is safe to say that war correspondents are commonly, although not necessarily in all cases, equated with so-called "embedded journalists". In order to become a war

correspondent within the meaning of international humanitarian law, official accreditation by the armed forces is mandatory. Thus, if an "embedded journalist" has received the official accreditation, then legally he is a war correspondent.*

Faulkner had concluded his report with a paragraph from a comprehensive article by Hans-Peter Gasser, a former senior legal advisor with the International Committee of the Red Cross:

> If they [journalists] are too close to the "heat of battle", or if they travel with a military unit, ride in a military vehicle or wear clothing similar to a military uniform, they do not lose their legal right to protection as a civilian, but such protection is de facto no longer possible... They accept the danger and act at their own risk. Any person who happens to be too close to a military object may at any moment come under enemy fire. Journalists who wear a uniform or some similar clothing may actually become a military target, not by right but because they fail to identify themselves as civilians: they just look like ordinary soldiers.

---

* International Committee of the Red Cross (online), 27th July 2010: 'How Does International Humanitarian Law Protect Journalists in Armed Conflict?'

Outside the Wires

Whenever I was away from Bastion, away from the office, away from the Ops Watch laptop, I felt like I was outside the loop. Going to a patrol base was all well and good for seeing the war in close-up – it allowed you to zoom in – but you lost sight of everything else going on outside the frame. In the same way that Russ had needed a guide when he was filming out on the ground, I felt like I needed a guide to keep me informed about the rest of the war.

The evening of 25th June followed an increasingly familiar pattern for me. When all of my JMOC colleagues went off to dinner, I stayed behind and manned the phones. That meant I took up my position at the Ops Watch laptop and looked through all the significant events of the day.

In the last hour a US Marine brought into Bastion with facial wounds had gone into cardiac arrest. His unit – 2nd Battalion 8th Marines – had come under fire from insurgents during a security operation in Nad-e Ali, leaving one Marine with a gunshot wound to the right shoulder and another with gunshot wounds to the left foot and buttock. The rest of the Marines had retaliated with small-arms fire and a 40-mm grenade launcher; in the resulting confusion, one of the grenades had apparently landed short, leaving two Marines with serious shrapnel wounds to the face (both Cat A). All of the wounded had been flown back to Bastion, where the Marine who had suffered a heart attack had just died.

Elsewhere in Afghanistan, an insurgent with a car bomb had tried to enter the Police Headquarters in Logar's Azrah District. After being denied entry, he drove the vehicle into a nearby hospital and detonated the device, killing twenty Afghan civilians and leaving twenty-three wounded.

This incident had made it into the news, with the BBC putting the death toll at twenty-seven, making it the worst attack against a medical facility in Afghanistan since 2001. A member of the Logar provincial council told a reporter: "It is no less than a Doomsday. The government and its intelligent agencies should have been able to prevent this. To the enemies of the people and Islam, I say, what do you get from a bloodbath like this?"

The next day was very much the same – more boredom and more horror. The 9th/12th Royal Lancers got hit just before lunchtime, an insurgent throwing a grenade into one of A Squadron's Jackals during a mounted patrol. Luckily, no one was killed. Three Lancers were classed as Cat C, with one of them being flown into Bastion with significant hearing loss, lower back pain and signs of battle shock. According to the report, this was his "third involvement with an explosion/near miss".

At the brief that evening, Faulkner gave us the number of significant acts for the day – 127* – then introduced Harriet's replacement. Sarah had just arrived at the JMOC and was going to be working alongside Harriet for the next week, learning the ropes. She was one of the palest women I had ever seen, her skin colour much closer to ivory than pink.

"I really don't like the sun," she admitted.

My own replacement – a young captain called Joe – was arriving in a week. He worked alongside Russ at the Media and

---

* See Appendix 1: Field Reports and Significant Acts.

Communications team at the British Army's headquarters in Andover. I'd met him once on a trip to see Russ just prior to our deployment, and he seemed like a good guy. He would be landing at about the same time I got back from Kabul.

My flight out to Kabul – due the next morning – was delayed because of technical problems. The long-suffering Hercules needed some extra care and attention, so the check-in time had been pushed back to the evening. With nothing else to do, I spent the afternoon tidying my room, getting it ready for Joe so he could move in straight away. I left my rug that I'd bought from one of the Afghan shops on camp, plus a cheap set of iPod docks I'd picked up at the NAAFI, and moved the rest of my stuff – the kit that I wasn't taking to Kabul – into a spare bed space in the transit tent.

Mick drove me over to the Passenger Handling Facility later that evening. I was carrying an improbable amount of kit, weighed down with the camera and tripod in addition to all my usual clobber. The holding area was busy, but not uncomfortably so. Most of my fellow passengers – a mixture of soldiers, civil servants and reporters – filled a bank of seats in front of a large flatscreen television that was showing one of the quarter-finals at Wimbledon. I threw my kit down near the back of the room and watched the match over the top of their heads.

We eventually left at just after 10 p.m., the good old Hercules creaking and groaning through the skies at 30,000 feet before landing at Kabul Airport at 23.30, coming to a halt alongside a gleaming-white private jet that was parked right outside the terminal. Obviously someone very important was either just arriving or just leaving. Four security guards in dark suits were standing by the jet as we walked past, ensuring none of us got too close.

I had my own security detail waiting for me on the other side of the terminal. Two guys from G4S threw my kit into the back of their Land Cruiser and sped me to the Embassy. There was no Scott tonight – he was back in the UK on leave. Instead I got Joshua, a lean, bearded diplomat in his late twenties, waiting for me at the front gates.

"The graduation ceremony is now taking place on Wednesday," he told me as we walked through the gardens to my villa. "You've got tomorrow off."

He showed me to my room. It was on the ground floor, right next to the kitchen. One side of it was taken up with a huge window that looked out onto the garden. A door in the window opened onto a small terrace, separated from the garden by a four-foot wall.

"It's perfect, Joshua."

"I'm fairly busy at the moment, but I'll catch up with you at breakfast on Wednesday."

As soon as Joshua left, I went into the deserted kitchen and checked the fridge for beer. There were a couple of bottles of wine, but no lager. I had been really looking forward to an ice-cold Heineken hitting my lips. I went round the kitchen, checking all the cupboards, but found nothing. Out of desperation, I checked the fridge again, this time looking in the vegetable compartment.

I found a can of Stella inside a bag of carrots. Not a bad hiding place, really. It was already fairly cold, but I put it in the freezer section anyway – standard operating procedure – and went for a shower.

After my shower – which was glorious – I padded through the kitchen in my towel, extracted the Stella from the freezer, and returned to my room. I switched on the TV and flicked through all the channels. On one of them, *2001: A Space Odyssey* was just starting. I lay on my bed and watched the apes going at it for twenty minutes, just about finishing my beer before I fell asleep.

I woke at 6.30 the following morning. A large tree shaded my window, but I could see the garden already bathed in sunlight. I went over to the window, my towel slipping from my waist as I stepped through the door onto the terrace. There was no one about, and I liked the feel of the cool, morning air all over my body. I yawned loudly and stretched up my arms.

"Good morning, sir."

A Gurkha with a machine gun was standing in front of me, right on the other side of my little wall. They patrolled the gardens in their smart blue uniforms and caps.

I cleared my throat. "Good morning."

I stepped back into my room and drew the curtains. It was good to know the Gurkhas were out there, but they didn't need to see me naked. No one benefited from that. I climbed back into bed and went to sleep again.

I woke up two hours later. It was 8.40 a.m. I had just enough time to shave, put on my uniform and walk over to the canteen. The staff were already clearing the hotplates when I got there, so I settled for a bowl of Weetabix, a plate of fruit (melon, apple, kiwi) and a glass of pineapple juice.

After breakfast I walked over to the Embassy shop – it was a well-stocked Portakabin outside the canteen – and bought twelve cans of Heineken, plus a can of Stella to replace the one I took. I went back to the villa, put the beers in the fridge and changed into my grey hooded top and shorts. Then I headed for the pool.

The next eight hours were taken up with sunbathing and swimming. I had the pool to myself for most of the day. The odd diplomat came in for a dip or to catch some sun, but they didn't stay long. They had work to do, clearly.

I didn't see any sign of Joshua at dinner. I ate my rump steak on my own, watching Wimbledon on the big flatscreen at the back of the canteen.

I walked back to my room after dinner to the faint sound of sirens. This was Kabul's soundtrack, wailing through its chaotic streets three or four times a day. Somewhere in the city, yet another very bad thing had just happened.

In the villa I took a Heineken from the fridge and sat in the empty lounge. I still hadn't seen any of my housemates. I flicked through the movie channels on the TV, before settling on a DVD box set of *Generation Kill*.

I slept soundly again that night – safe inside the Embassy bubble – then went to breakfast for 8 a.m., ready to do some filming. I bumped into Joshua just as he was coming out the door.

"The graduation ceremony is tomorrow now," he said. "I'm really sorry. Is that going to be a problem?"

"Not really, no."

I ate my breakfast, then spent another day by the pool.

* * *

During my peaceful mini-break, the Intercontinental Hotel, about twenty minutes' drive down the road, was attacked by insurgents. It happened on the Tuesday night, around the time I was returning to my villa after dinner. Although the attack was widely reported throughout the world, I knew nothing about it until the Thursday morning, when I was chatting to Steve, one of the G4S guys who were taking me and Joshua to the Staff College.

"We'll be going past the Intercontinental Hotel this morning," he said. "It's right next to the Staff College."

"I'm quite curious to see that," said Joshua. "See what the damage is."

"The damage?" I said. "What happened?"

Steve explained. A suicide bomber had run into the lobby and blown himself up. At least five insurgents had then run in, firing AK-47s. Ten civilians – mostly hotel workers – died in the attack. Afghan security forces, helped by members of the New Zealand SAS, surrounded the hotel. The ensuing firefight had lasted several hours before the remaining insurgents were killed.

"It's the standard way the insurgents do it now," said Steve. "Send the suicide bomber in, then follow it up with small-arms fire."

At least two of the insurgents made it up to the hotel roof, only to be blown to pieces by a NATO helicopter. This started a fire that was captured on film and broadcast by countless international news outlets. We saw the damage from the road as we drove past, the flames having gutted one half of the top floor.

The Staff College, at least, was untouched. We arrived there ten minutes before the graduation ceremony was due to start, but the guards on the gate, still jumpy over the hotel attack, kept us waiting for fifteen minutes while they ran a number of pointless security checks. By the time we got into the main headquarters, the ceremony had begun. All the officers on the course were sitting at their desks in the largest classroom on the top floor, listening to a speech by one of their senior commanders. He looked as old as the hills, his white beard and rumbling voice giving him the air of an Afghan Moses. I had no idea what he was saying, but I set up the camera on the tripod at the back of the room and started filming.

Following the speech, each officer was presented with a certificate. They had to march to the front of the room and shake hands with the course instructors, all of whom had gathered under a portrait of the Afghan President Hamid Karzai. I took the camera off the tripod and filmed them from a number of different angles, always trying to frame each officer in the same shot as the British instructors I'd already interviewed. The plan was to put together a series of pieces for regional TV, each centred on a British instructor local to that region.

After the ceremony, I tried to get an interview with the senior commander who'd given the speech, but he left almost immediately, apparently suspicious of the media. I'd already interviewed a number of officers on the course, but I still needed something from a senior Afghan figure to give an overview of the training. As well as British regional television, I was hoping to send the footage to some of the stations in Kabul in an effort to strengthen our links with the Afghan media.

"The best man to interview is Major General Patang," said Joshua. "But he tends to be quite busy."

Major General Patang was the head of the Afghan National Police Training General Command. In other words, he ran the whole show. If I could get an interview with him, the Afghan stations would come knocking.

"Can we get him?"

"Not today," said Joshua. "We'll have to come back again. What's your schedule like? You could be stuck at the Embassy for a few days."

I interviewed Major General Patang three days later. In the meantime, I just did what you do when you're stuck at the Embassy for a few days. I drank all the Heinekens, drank some Carlsberg, watched a lot of movies, ate some nice meals, swam many lengths of the pool and got very brown. As holidays in Afghanistan go, it wasn't that bad.

The day after the Patang interview, I was supposed to catch my rescheduled flight to Bastion – which, however, was cancelled due to technical problems. I waited at the airport for an hour before the announcement came through. The Hercules would not be flying for another twenty-four hours, which meant I would be spending another night in the Embassy. A G4S team came back to pick me up.

"You might get to see the big man," said the driver. "He's just arrived at the Embassy."

"Which big man?"

"The Prime Minister."

"Our Prime Minister?"

David Cameron was in town, preparing to make an announcement about a planned withdrawal of British forces. His original timetable was supposed to take him to Lashkar Gah, but the mysterious disappearance of a British soldier in Nahr-e Saraj had thrown out his schedule, every available helicopter being pulled into the search. The Prime Minister had flown straight into Bastion, met some of the troops, then flown up to Kabul for a night at the Embassy.

I did not get to see him by the pool the following morning. He went straight to the Presidential Palace for talks with Hamid Karzai, before flying back to the UK in the evening. The next day he gave a statement to the House of Commons, announcing that British troop levels in Afghanistan would drop from 9,500 to 9,000 by the end of 2012.

* * *

I finally got back to Bastion on the afternoon of Tuesday 5th July, leaving me just eight days and a wake-up until my flight home. My replacement, Joe, had by now arrived at the JMOC and settled into my old bed space. I'd planned to spend my last few days conducting a handover with him, but he had other ideas. He'd brought a civilian cameraman with him from the British Army's Media and Communication Team, and was shooting footage and interviews for a BBC series called *How to Go to War*. I would have to fit the handover around his filming schedule.

By this stage, I wasn't particularly bothered any more. Like most soldiers nearing the end of their tour, I was just focused on going home. To all intents and purposes, I was already sitting on my Tristar, flying away from Afghanistan for ever.

Faulkner went through his usual roll call of death and destruction at the brief that evening, although even among all the carnage there was some cause for optimism.

"Ninety-nine significant acts today," he said. "Which is forty-five per cent down on what it was this time last year. So although it's the fighting season, there hasn't been that much fighting."

I sat in the corner of the office, wondering whether I'd spent the last four months in some twisted parallel universe. A man at a desk was reading numbers off a page, saying there hadn't been much fighting. He was not wrong – the summer had been quieter than recent years – but it still felt completely fucked up.

"We killed 164 insurgents across theatre this week," he said. "Thirty-eight captured or detained."

He then told us more about a British soldier whose body had been found after he went missing from his base in Nahr-e Saraj. Highlander Scott McLaren from 4 Scots had inexplicably walked out of Salaang on his own in the early hours of Monday morning. The twenty-year-old's disappearance had triggered a seventeen-hour search operation involving hundreds of troops across Nahr-e Saraj. His body was eventually discovered in a culvert around 700 metres north-east of Patrol Base 4.

"There's all sorts of speculation about what happened," Faulkner said. "But we still don't know. It's still under investigation."

Colonel Lucas had already issued a statement to the media to that effect, which had been reproduced in most of the main British newspapers. This hadn't stopped the press from coming up with a number of theories about his disappearance and death. The *Daily Telegraph* quoted a "top Afghan commander for the province", Sayed Maluk. He said that McLaren had been found dead in a stream that ran through his base after apparently drowning, and his body was later shot by insurgents.* Meanwhile, the *Telegraph*'s Toby Harnden suggested that Highlander McLaren's actions were possibly the result of "battle shock".† Later in the week, the *Sunday Times* claimed to have spoken to one of the insurgents responsible for Highlander McLaren's death. The paper reported that the twenty-year-old had fallen into the hands of a group of Taliban fighters who had tortured and shot him. It claimed their commanders later rewarded them for their efforts with a motorbike and the equivalent of £180 in cash. "The senior leaders in Pakistan were very happy with us," one of them apparently told the newspaper.‡ On the same day, the *Sunday Telegraph* published the findings of its own investigation, claiming that Highlander McLaren had left Salaang to find a pair of night-vision goggles.§

---

* *Daily Telegraph* (online), 5th July 2011: 'UK Soldier in Afghanistan "Drowned after Going for a Swim"'.
† *Daily Telegraph* (online, Toby Harnden blog): '5th July 2011: Highlander Scott McLaren and the Toll of Battle Shock'.
‡ *The Sunday Times*, 10th July 2011: 'Taliban Fighters Get Bikes for Killing British Soldier'.
§ *The Sunday Telegraph*, 10th July 2011: 'British Soldier Missing for Two Hours before Alarm Was Raised'.

This version of events came closest to the findings of the inquest into his death in December 2011, which recorded a verdict of unlawful killing after he was captured by insurgents, tortured and shot in the head. It heard that McLaren went to retrieve the goggles – considered a vital piece of kit – after they'd been left behind by another soldier at a nearby vehicle checkpoint. However, when he walked out of Salaang at 2 a.m., he was caught on CCTV heading straight past the bridge that led to the checkpoint. The coroner at his inquest said: "Quite clearly, Scott was concerned as regards the missing goggles and talked of going back to the checkpoint on the northern side of the canal where they were last seen. The evidence, in particular the CCTV imagery, points quite clearly to Scott heading in the direction of the bridge. But he never crosses the bridge and heads off in an entirely different direction. It is unclear what Scott was doing that night, and sadly the only person who could help us is no longer with us."

A Hazardous Environment

On the day I returned from Kabul, four newly arrived reporters were undergoing their Media Induction Package at Bastion. In terms of readiness, they had not made a great first impression on the JMOC. Faulkner shared his concerns about their dress and equipment with the rest of the office the morning after their arrival.

"One turned up in some baggy, low-crotch harem pants," he muttered. "She insisted they were perfect for hot places."

He was drafting a lengthy email to PJHQ, calling for a more comprehensive training programme for embedded journalists. Three of the four had attended the MoD-run "Hazardous Environment Course" back in the UK, but apparently it was lacking in useful information.

"They said there was an interesting lecture on how the Chinese recruit sleeper agents," Faulkner said. "But that was about it."

It being a war zone, he soon had other stuff to distract him. An RAF Reaper had blown up two trucks in Now Zad, successfully killing two insurgents and inadvertently killing four Afghan civilians. Sky News was running a report on the incident, describing it – not incorrectly – as a "drone" strike.*

"We don't say 'drone' any more," Faulkner said, reading back through the MoD's official statement. "It's a remotely piloted air system."

---

* Sky News (online), 6th July 2011: 'Four Afghan Civilians Killed by RAF Drone'.

I wondered whether "drone" was such a terrible word. To my ears it spoke of something dull and inert, bringing to mind the ramblings of a dinner-party bore. It certainly wasn't as disturbing as "Reaper" – the name provided by the US manufacturers – which brought up the classic image of Death himself, scythe in hand, looming over his next victim.

At just after midday a flight lieutenant called Simon walked in. He was the RAF's media-liaison officer in Kandahar, come to visit us on a whim. His admin sergeant – a squat man with beady eyes – had travelled with him. He'd picked up some "Kill TV" along the way, and thought we might like to see it.

"I've got the file here," he said, holding up a USB stick. "It's awesome."

None of us leapt up to join him. He sat at the desk recently vacated by Russ, opening the video file on the spare computer. Only Simon stood behind him, looking over his shoulder.

"It's from a Tornado using Brimstone,"* said the sergeant, unperturbed by the general lack of enthusiasm in the room. "They'd spotted a dicker† on top of a hill. You can just about see his mobile phone."

Simon leant forward, squinting at the footage. "I can't see anything."

"Hang on." The sergeant mouse-clicked a few times, trying to sharpen up the grainy image of the insurgent. "How about now?"

"What's that?" Simon said.

"That's the impact."

Simon took his time. "I still don't know what I'm looking at."

---

*   Air-to-ground missiles used by RAF Tornados. Not to be confused with the counter-IED teams also known as Brimstone.

†   An observer reporting troop movements to the insurgents.

The sergeant clicked again. "When you switch to infrared, you can clearly see blood spurting out of him."

Again Simon squinted at the screen. "It's still not clear..."

The sergeant sighed heavily. "Once you establish what you're looking at, it's clear. His head and a trail of blood go in one direction, and his torso and a different trail of blood go in another direction. His legs stay where they are."

Simon grimaced. "Did we release this?"

"No," snapped Faulkner from across the room. He'd already had enough of the pair. "We don't do snuff movies."

We had just one more visitor that day. An Apache pilot dropped off some cockpit footage just before dinner. His clips highlighted some brilliant tactical flying, but alas, there were no kills in the picture.

"We used to kill forty to fifty insurgents a week," he said casually. "It's gone down now."

That was how he talked about it. Like the unexcitable slaughter of insurgents was the norm.

Which it was, of course.

* * *

A day after completing the Media Induction Package, one of the newly arrived reporters – Stephen Bailey – flew out to Patrol Base 2 to join C Company of 1 Rifles. Tom, the huge commando from TFH who normally made the tea for Colonel Lucas, accompanied him. Having learnt of his growing frustration with life in the office, Colonel Lucas had allowed his admin sergeant to try his hand at the job of media minder, escorting the journalist out on the ground.

As a physical specimen, Stephen did not look like someone who would take naturally to a foot patrol in the Green Zone. Skinny and bespectacled, he seemed almost too human alongside Tom, who looked not unlike a Norse god.

At 16.30, the two of them left the base as part of a joint 1 Rifles/ANA patrol. Stephen was nervous. He'd never been to Afghanistan before, and this was his first time outside the wire. He'd already spoken to Tom about some of his fears, which centred around IEDs, small-arms fire and heat illness.

"He did ask a lot of questions," Tom told us later, sitting in the JMOC. "I tried to answer them in a reassuring manner."

The aim of the patrol was to set up a vehicle checkpoint about 600 metres from the base. The ANA would be conducting the checkpoint itself, while the soldiers from 1 Rifles would provide cover. They expected to be out on the ground for about three hours.

The patrol headed out along a tarmac road leading from the base, watched by a number of local women and children in nearby compounds. The area was home to several families, and the patrol had to stop several times to allow traffic to pass. Tom used these moments to check up on Stephen.

"I'm OK," Stephen said. "Just hot."

Tom felt this was quite normal – everyone was hot, it was still in the mid-thirties – so they carried on.

After 500 metres the patrol split in two. The Afghans continued along the tarmac road, while the Rifles turned onto a track that led through a series of rundown compounds.

Two hundred metres down that track, the Rifles stopped and carried out a counter-IED drill. Tom noticed that Stephen was beginning to struggle with the heat and told him to sit down and drink some water.

Stephen did as he was told, but he was still having problems. Within a few minutes, it was clear he was experiencing the initial stages of heat illness: clammy skin, faintness, light shaking.

By now, the patrol had been out on the ground for just over half an hour. Tom spoke to the patrol commander, and the decision was taken for the Rifles to return with Stephen to Patrol Base 2.

They began moving back towards the road, Tom with one arm under Stephen, supporting him. Another soldier also helped. Stephen's condition was deteriorating: he was very weak and faint, garbling his words.

When they got to the road, Tom picked up Stephen and started to carry him. He managed to cover about 150 metres before Stephen told him to stop.

"I feel sick," he mumbled.

Tom stopped and stood him up in the road. They were still some distance from the patrol base, but there was a small ANP checkpoint less than a hundred metres away.

"I'll walk," said Stephen.

He began to walk towards the ANP checkpoint, Tom and another soldier either side of him. After a few steps, he collapsed and started fitting.

"I was directly beside him and delivered immediate first aid," Tom recalled. "I rolled him onto his side into the recovery position, which proved difficult because of how rigorously his muscles were contracting. The main concern was his airway, which had fully closed because his neck muscles were pulling his chin down onto his chest, while his tongue had retracted into his throat. He was frothing at the mouth and had not drawn breath for at least thirty seconds while I wrestled to force an airway. At this stage he had gone blue and was clearly in trouble. I forced my knee into the base of his neck and counter-levered his forehead to open his airway. He then proceeded

236

to projectile-vomit a mixture of blood and water from his mouth and nose. This continued sporadically for about five minutes."

As this was going on, the Rifles went into all-round defence. They were dangerously exposed on the road, and the atmospherics were not good. Within the last few minutes, all the women and children in the area had disappeared from view.

"The area was not secure," Tom said. "Further casualties would've caused tremendous problems. I was not going to let that happen."

Tom ripped off Stephen's body armour. Other members of the patrol started pouring their water over his body, trying to cool him down. They strapped him to a stretcher and carried him the rest of the way to the ANP checkpoint, where a Mastiff from Patrol Base 2 met them.

"When we got into the Mastiff, space was tight. Stephen could not fit into the vehicle comfortably. In order to shut the back doors, he had to be moved as far forward as possible, which caused his head to raise up and his airway to close. I grabbed his belt buckle and pulled him hard towards me, which caused his head to drop back again."

In the medical centre at Patrol Base 2, Stephen was still fitting. It took several soldiers to hold him down while one of the medics applied an intravenous drip.

"It was a struggle to keep any lines or oxygen in or on him due to his convulsions," Tom said. "But the medics, who clearly had a lot of experience with heat casualties, were able to help him."

Stephen's body temperature began to lower and he started to regain consciousness. A US "Pedro" medevac helicopter was called in, landing at Patrol Base 2 twenty minutes later. The Pedro medics sedated Stephen and flew him straight back to the hospital at Bastion.

Stephen stayed in the hospital at Bastion for three days, during which time he'd recovered enough to write a feature on his experience for the *Bournemouth Echo*:

> The doctors told me I had a temperature of 41° C, that my blood tests were "deranged", and that I was the worst case of heat illness they've had this year.[*]

He was then flown back to the UK and spent four days in Birmingham's Queen Elizabeth Hospital before being discharged. During his time there he wrote another feature on the incident, thanking all those who saved him:

> I will always remember the professionalism and care of the people who helped me from a dusty Afghan roadside all the way back to a fifth-floor hospital ward in Birmingham.[†]

In his weekly report following the incident, Faulkner repeated his calls for PJHQ to implement a more comprehensive training programme for embedded journalists. He drew heavily on Tom's account of the incident with Stephen, even though the unflappable commando was keen to play down his heroics.

"Ultimately it was the patrol commander and his men who saved Stephen's life," Tom said. "I simply happened to be stood right beside him because of the nature of my job."

---

[*]   *Bournemouth Echo* (online), 9th July 2011: '*Echo* Journalist in Black Hawk Rescue'.

[†]   *Bournemouth Echo* (online), 16th July 2011: 'Reporter Pays Tribute to Armed Forces after Being Taken Ill in Afghanistan'.

Last Legs

On the same day that Stephen Bailey nearly died, another 1 Rifles patrol, this one from A Company, conducted a security operation just outside Salaang. As they crossed the corner of a ploughed field south-east of the base, an IED detonated. One of the Rifles lost both his legs below the knees, and one of his arms below the elbow.

Elsewhere in Nahr-e Saraj, Danish soldiers from 2 Armoured Infantry Company were out on a foot patrol when they stopped for a moment alongside a wall. As they rested, an insurgent on the other side of the wall threw two mortar rounds at them, fashioned as hand grenades. The resulting blasts left three of the Danes Cat A and three Cat B. They were flown to Bastion with a variety of fragmentation wounds to their arms and legs.

"102 significant acts today," Faulkner said that evening. "It's gone up slightly."

As per usual, it was all about the numbers. Away from the eyes of the media, that was how we measured the tempo of the war. That was our report, the only one that counted.

The next day the number of significant acts fell to eighty-five. It kept falling through the weekend, and by Tuesday it was down to forty-two.

"The figures are looking good at the moment," Faulkner said that evening. "114 insurgents killed in the last week. 224 detained. Also Nad-e Ali is showing a fifty-per-cent drop in significant acts year-on-year. And the number of locals coming forward and reporting the locations of IEDs has gone up by sixty-eight per cent."

It wasn't all good news. Even when the number of significant acts was low, the hospital at Bastion was kept busy. That lunchtime a joint foot patrol from 215th ANA Corps and 2nd Battalion 8th US Marines struck an IED in Sangin, leaving one Marine with Cat A blast wounds. Two hours later a foot patrol from 1st Battalion 5th US Marines struck another IED in Sangin, resulting in another Cat A Marine. Back at Bastion, he died from his wounds. Four hours later, a joint patrol from 215th ANA Corps and 3rd Battalion 2nd US Marines came under small-arms fire in Now Zad, leaving two Marines Cat A. They were also flown back to Bastion, where one of them later died

Outside Helmand, meanwhile, there was bad news coming out of Kandahar. Ahmad Wali Karzai – the half-brother of President Karzai and a leading power-broker in the south of the country – had been shot dead by a man described as his "head of security". The Taliban had issued a statement claiming responsibility, their spokesman Zabiullah Mujahid calling it one of their greatest achievements in ten years of war. Doubts had been raised about the Taliban's claims, however, amid rumours the killing had been fuelled by a personal grudge. Unfortunately the gunman's exact motives were difficult to establish, as he'd been shot dead by another security guard almost immediately.

"We think Ahmad Karzai's death could cause a few problems," Faulkner said. "Intelligence are talking about a destabilizing power struggle."

He moved on to media-related matters. Miles Amoore had written a less than flattering article on the state of the ANA following his short stay with 1 Rifles the previous week. It had run in the *Sunday Times* with a quote from one of the Rifles officers: "Without us cajoling, pushing or pleading, the Afghan army would sit on their arse and do fuck all."*

"It's outrageous," Faulkner said.

"Not good at all," added Dougie.

The article described an operation by 1 Rifles in Nahr-e Saraj back in May. Soldiers from A Company had come under fire while occupying a compound in the village of Alikozai. Amoore had written up the piece following his recent stay with the Rifles at Patrol Base 2. His style of reporting was not dissimilar to Virginia Wheeler's, full of punchy, vivid detail:

> The bullet tore into the British sniper's hip and knocked him to the ground. Surrounded by Taliban fighters after being pinned down by heavy fire inside a mud compound for seven hours, British soldiers suffering from heat exhaustion dragged the wounded corporal from the rooftop and into an inner courtyard.

"It's overly graphic for no apparent reason," Faulkner said. "He wasn't there, how would he know? It's just him repeating other people's stories."

The article had then shifted its focus onto the relative merits of the Afghan soldiers:

> There is a growing realization among British officers that the end result will not be perfect. The British have begun to call the outcome "Afghan good enough".

---

* *The Sunday Times*, 10th July 2011: 'British Push Afghans to Keep Taliban at Bay'.

"If they want to piss in the showers, smoke hash, blow the generator, refuse to wear helmets on patrol, then so be it," a British officer said.

At least Faulkner didn't hate all journalists. Mick had just returned from the flight line, where he'd dropped off a handful of reporters from the West Midlands.

"They wanted me to pass their thanks on to everyone," Mick said. "They said they'd been really well looked after."

"That's the way it goes," Faulkner said. "Some of the media have been complete arsewipes, and some have been brilliant. You just have to suck it all up."

I was due to fly home with Faulkner the following afternoon, both our tours ending on the same day. I had been hoping to relax as soon as I boarded the Tristar, but I had visions of Faulkner sitting next to me, lecturing me for hours on the warped duality of the media. It didn't help that we had to stop halfway in Cyprus for a mandatory twenty-four-hour decompression package. That meant sitting on the beach with him all afternoon before moving into the bar. Neither of us knew anybody else on the flight, so it had all the makings of a very long journey home.

* * *

Ahead of my last night in the JMOC, I learnt that Russ was not coming back. The compassionate cell back in the UK had deemed the condition of his close relative so serious that he was to remain in the UK. The Media and Communications Team at Andover was now trying to find a replacement who could fly out as soon as possible. Realistically, however, we were unlikely to get anyone for at least another fortnight.

Meanwhile Ali was on her way home, flying back for two weeks of R&R. I said goodbye to her outside the office, giving her a hug.

"It's been a pleasure working with you," I told her.

She laughed. "You don't mean that, boss!"

"Of course I do." I did as well. "Make sure Joe looks after you."

I'd hardly seen anything of Joe over the last week. He'd been glued to his cameraman every day since their arrival, working all over Bastion. When they weren't filming, Joe went straight to the gym, determined to pump himself up. He was already pretty trim, but he still felt the need for a daily workout.

"He can't wait to get out on the ground," said Ali.

"That's what worries me," I said. "Don't let him do anything daft."

I felt guilty saying goodbye to her. She still had six weeks to push when she got back from R&R. If Joe was desperate for action, then she would soon find herself back in harm's way.

"I'll be fine," said Ali. "See you at the next training weekend."

I waved Ali off, then went to my final evening brief. It was taken by Faulkner's replacement, a pint-sized wing commander called Baxter.

"Eighty-eight significant acts today," he mumbled, reading slowly from his notes. "So it's more than doubled from yesterday."

The worst incident had taken place in Kapisa, where French soldiers had been guarding a shura between tribal leaders. A suicide bomber had walked up to the soldiers as they stood by their armoured vehicles and detonated his explosives. The blast had killed five of the soldiers and left four with serious injuries.

"But there is some good news today," said Baxter, suddenly sitting up. "The insurgents behind Highlander McLaren's death have been killed. They were a four-man team, apparently. I can't tell you much more than that. Just that we got them about two kilometres from where he was found."

* * *

I said goodbye to my colleagues in the JMOC the following afternoon. Harriet had left while I was in Kabul, so it was only really Dougie and Mick.

"Hang in there, Dougie," I said.

He gave me a wry smile. "They're letting me go home in September now," he said. "I'm getting a month off for good behaviour."

"How about you, Mick?"

"Back in November."

"November?"

He nodded. "They're letting me go home for Christmas."

Faulkner and I got a lift to the Passenger Handling Facility, where we checked in our bags and weapons. Away from the JMOC, on his way home after six months staring at a computer screen in the middle of desert, he was in a good mood. We drank coffee in the holding area, chatting about home and all the things we were going to do on leave. The time passed surprisingly quickly.

We got separated as we boarded the Tristar. I found myself in a window seat over the wing, looking out towards the control tower. We sat on the tarmac for a good long time, waiting for something, I don't know what. By the time we took off, it was dark. When I looked down at Bastion for the last time, all I could see was a big constellation of lights, disappearing into the night.

Getting up into the air, I felt more relief than happiness. I'd dreamt about this moment for weeks, thinking I'd want to shout out with joy, but now it was happening, I was suddenly conscious of all the other soldiers and Marines around me. Some of them had done proper tours, spent months in the Green Zone, risking their lives every day, seeing their best friends killed or maimed. Who was I to celebrate around these men?

It was quiet on the plane. Every man was lost in his thoughts. Pretty soon the hypnotic drone of the engines took its toll. I closed my eyes and gave in easily to sleep.

We landed at Akrotiri four hours later, just as the sun was coming up. Time to decompress. All of us just wanted to go home, but this package was mandatory. It was supposed to reintroduce us to the comforts of civilian life (i.e. alcohol) in a controlled environment. Given my week at the British Embassy, I was hardly in desperate need of the sun loungers and the free booze, but I shuffled off the plane along with everybody else. Some buses took us to a place called Bloodhound Camp, where we showered, ate breakfast, then went to the beach. I wasn't normally one for swimming in the sea, but the sight of all that water was difficult to resist. I spent an hour just swimming around in circles under the watchful eye of a lifeguard in a kayak. He was just one of a dozen safety staff who tried to ensure that no one drowned.*

They gave us our beer tokens later that night. We were allowed four cans each. In recent years it had always been five cans, but then a platoon of Paras, heading home after a particularly difficult tour, took all their clothes off in the bar, horrifying the staff, who felt the fifth can was to blame.

We had a barbecue and watched a band perform on a small stage next to the bar. I worked my way through my beer allocation and

---

* A young gunner from the RAF Regiment had died during decompression the previous November, after he was hit by a power boat while swimming.

chatted to Faulkner. We had nothing in common, but it didn't matter. We were both just glad be going home.

We all slept in a big dormitory full of bunk beds. Reveille was at 3.15 a.m., but no one complained. We got dressed and got back on the buses and returned to the air terminal. It was just starting to get light when we walked across the tarmac to the Tristar. There were no delays this time. We all took our seats and the pilot said good morning and turned it around and took us all the way back to Brize Norton.

It was raining as we landed. The good old rain, the life-giving rain. It slanted across my window as I looked out over the fields of Oxfordshire. I hadn't seen it fall for more than four months.

The pilot parked us right outside the terminal. We all got off, exposing our sun-darkened faces to the rain as we stepped down onto the tarmac. As with our departure from Bastion, there was very little talking.

We walked into the terminal – a grey, squat building – and waited for our baggage. It came round on a carousel after five minutes. Our weapons came in separately. Each of us took a luggage trolley and made our way through to the lobby.

I saw one tearful reunion, a blonde wrapping herself around a stunned airman, but otherwise the lobby was empty. For some reason, I'd been expecting a mass outpouring of emotion, families throwing themselves at us as we appeared in the doorway, but that didn't happen. It seemed that most of us, like myself, had a little bit farther to go.

Faulkner came over. His lift was outside, and it was time to say goodbye.

"Take care, Christian. Good working with you."

"And you too, sir."

We smiled and shook hands, and that was that. He was gone. Whether he really thought it was good working with me, I had no idea. Possibly he thought I was one of the arsewipes, but didn't want to say.

My own transport turned up ten minutes later. It was the dreaded white minibus from Chilwell. Mercifully, the prostitute-loving corporal was nowhere to be seen. A sensible-looking civilian with grey hair was behind the wheel instead.

It took two hours to get back to Chilwell – the normal journey time. The sensible civilian dropped me off outside the armoury. I'd rung my father on the way back, giving him a pick-up time. He still hadn't arrived when we got there, so I had time to give my rifle and pistol a quick wipe-down before signing them back into the armoury.

When I stepped outside the armoury again, my father was just getting out of his car. He'd come straight from his weekly game of tennis, still wearing his shorts and a polo shirt. He smiled when he saw me, then broke into tears.

"Christian. Good to see you again."

I gave him a hug. "Hello, Dad."

"How are you?"

"I'm fine, Dad. I'm absolutely fine."

He drove home, telling me all his latest news: his tennis result (he won), a spat with the neighbours about a fence, Monty and Trudie's latest antics. I was keen to hear all about it. We stayed off the subject of Afghanistan for most of the journey.

"How was it out there?" he asked eventually.

"It was fine," I said. "Nothing bad happened."

"Really?"

"Well, not that I saw."

He nodded. "Good."

We got home, pulling up on the gravel driveway. A "Welcome Home" banner hung over the front door. As I climbed out of the car, the door opened and the dogs ran out. I had been concerned that Monty would have a heart attack on seeing me – he was ten years old and showing it – but he was quite well behaved, as was Trudie (two years old, not a heart-attack risk). They both stopped in front of me and waited to be fussed over, tails wagging. I'd instructed my mother to show them home-video footage of me in the last few days so that my return wouldn't come as such a shock. It seemed to be working.

I knelt down and petted them both, just as the rest of my family came out: my mother, brother and sister, along with my three-year-old nephew Laurie. He hurried over first, excited to see his uncle in an army uniform. I picked him up and ruffled his hair, then walked over to my mother.

"Hello, Mum."

I had expected my mother to do some crying, but she was surprisingly composed. I began to think my father had somehow managed to shed all the tears on her behalf. She looked at me almost warily, as though she wasn't quite sure what to expect.

"How are you?" she asked.

"I'm fine, Mum." I put Laurie down and gave her a hug. "I'm just fine."

"Are you sure?"

At no stage had I told my parents I'd suffered in Afghanistan, but they were still clearly concerned that a traumatized monster might have returned in my place. My phone calls home had always been scant on working detail – the insecure lines meant that actual information had to be kept to a minimum – so their imaginations had filled in the gaps.

"I'm absolutely fine," I said. "Trust me."

My mother seemed happy with my answer, but I gave her another hug anyway. It was a day for hugging. My sister and brother were next – they got the treatment – then my mother suggested we all go into the house.

"We've got bubbly in the fridge," she said, tears filling her eyes.

"We better drink it then."

I followed them inside for champagne and sympathy, the former somewhat more deserved than the latter.

Epilogue

A year has passed since I returned from Afghanistan. I'm writing this at home in Nottinghamshire, the rain hammering against the loft window. After two very dry winters, we've had one of the wettest summers since records began. A lot of the country has been suffering from drought, so no one is really complaining. Hard rain is much needed.

The war drifts in and out of the news, struggling to make the headlines. "Afghanistan fatigue" doesn't just affect the troops: apparently it extends to the general public, tired of hearing about something so miserable, so far away. The appetite for tales of woe from the desert has been replaced by more domestic concerns, the Western media preferring to focus on crime, showbiz, the economy and the weather.

I haven't seen Russ since I got back – we're friends on Facebook, nothing more – but I saw Ali at an MOG training weekend back in November. She'd only been back a few weeks, her face still brown from the Afghan sun.

"How did the rest of it go?" I asked her.

"It was OK," she said. "We had a bit of fun with the Rifles, but it was all good."

I already knew about the Rifles operation. Joe had started pushing for places on the Afghan-led offensive in Nahr-e Saraj within days of his arrival. By all accounts the operation had gone well, although Joe and Ali had come under heavy fire while out on patrol.

"How was Joe?"

"Joe was good, although he changed after that contact."

"In what way?"

"Much less gung-ho. We didn't go out as much after that."

We chatted for ten minutes, reminiscing about the JMOC, running through the various personalities. Eventually we got around to some of the reporters, including the big man himself.

"Ross Kemp came back out," Ali said, "and the Taliban finally shot at him!"

I had to smile. "Thank God for that."

"An RPG as well. So he was happy."

I pictured Ross hurling himself into a ditch as the RPG streaked overhead. After all those weeks in the Green Zone, he'd finally got what he wanted. Not for him the second-hand war story. He had to be there, right on the receiving end.

I was very different. I didn't want to be there, right on the receiving end. I wanted to be somewhere else, somewhere safer.

As a BBC journalist and a reservist in the Media Operations Group, my priorities are easily blurred, but at least in the JMOC I had access to lines of communication that were clear and uncompromising. I occupied a privileged position, being able to look upon the war as both a soldier and a reporter. To my mind, that brought with it an obligation – moral, if not professional – to say something about what I saw.

The field reports might be considered a lame alternative to actual war reporting, but that doesn't bother me. As far as I'm concerned, they do the job. Whenever I was in the field, away from Ops Watch, I didn't know what was going on, save for the dramas in our own little tactical area. We'd be sitting in a patrol base, and Op Minimize would be announced, and no one would know why.

With the field reports at least, you knew what was happening. Throughout my tour I made a note of them whenever I could, and I've reproduced some of them in this book. Taken individually, they're just snapshots, offering nothing more than a glimpse into the routine miseries of war. Considered as a whole, however, they produce a more telling effect, their numbers growing all the time, their depth of field stretching into the distance. Like rows of headstones in a cemetery, their strength lies in their repetition – they do not lend themselves to desensitization, and they do not lose their power to shock.

Not that the Combat Camera Team was trying to shock anybody. Our name was always a misnomer. We weren't there to film and photograph combat. We were there to film and photograph something resembling its exact opposite. We were there to record evidence of progress.

Prior to Afghanistan, Combat Camera Teams were known as Mobile News Teams, but that didn't work. No fighting unit wanted to go out on the ground with a Mobile News Team – it sounded like a liability. A trio of media guys – uniform or no uniform – would just slow everybody down. Hence the name change, turning us into something more robust, something more self-sufficient; a team that could presumably handle itself in a combat environment and not get everybody else killed.

I didn't get the chance to describe combat first-hand, and for that I'm grateful. I've read enough of the reports to know it's not something I want inside my head. There's already enough stuff jumbling around in there as it is.

My career in local radio continues at a slow, inexorable pace, only now with the occasional panic attack. For almost ten years I've read the news and not been remotely bothered about any technical difficulties that might arise during the bulletin. At the BBC we read the news off a monitor using a system called Radioman, which occasionally crashes, forcing the reader to revert to a printed version of the bulletin. This has never derailed me in the past – why would it? – but now, when it happens, the attack kicks in. My pulse rate doubles in a matter of seconds: I can feel my face start to burn and, most disastrously, I start to gasp for air.

Naturally I can see the funny side – there is something inherently amusing about a newsreader having a panic attack during a bulletin – but it's never comical at the time. When it's actually happening, it feels like I'm having a heart attack.

It's happened three times since I got back from Afghanistan. Mercifully, it's always been the 6 a.m. bulletin, when perhaps Radioman is still half asleep, and when hardly anybody is listening. The first two times it happened near the end of the bulletin, and I managed to curtail the read without drawing too much attention to myself. The third time was much worse – it crashed on my first story. I practically stopped breathing, my attempts to read sounding like something out of a horror movie. Had any children been listening, it would've given them nightmares. After twenty seconds I couldn't take it any more, clawing at the faders, killing my microphone. The presenter had to cut back in, mumbling something about "technical difficulties" before playing a song.

My colleagues were perfectly good about it – they asked if I was OK, and then nothing more was said – but it's not something I can just ignore. I have no idea why it happens. I'm certainly not traumatized by my experiences in Afghanistan. As I always tell people, nothing bad happened to me out there.

I don't know. Maybe it's my mind's way of telling me to leave again and do something else – although, frankly, I have no idea what that would be.

APPENDIX 1

Field Reports and Significant Acts

TWO QUIET DAYS ON THE AFGHAN FRONT (25TH–26TH JUNE 2011)

Saturday 25th June 2011
Significant acts: N/A.

Helmand, 5.50 a.m.
A foot patrol from L Company 42 Commando comes under small-arms and indirect fire from up to three insurgents in Nahr-e Saraj. The Marines positively identify the insurgents' position and return fire with fifty mortar rounds. Two A-10s from the 74th US Expeditionary Fighter Squadron drop one GBU-38 500-lb bomb and one GBU-54 500-lb bomb. Two Apaches engage the insurgents with one AGM-114 (Hellfire) and five hundred and sixty 30-mm rounds, forcing them to withdraw. Later the patrol is re-engaged by between two and four insurgents with indirect fire. The two Apaches positively identify the insurgents inside a compound and engage them with one AGM-114 and five hundred and twenty 30-mm rounds, forcing them to break contact. The engagement results in two buildings destroyed, one building damaged, one wall damaged and two insurgents killed (unconfirmed). There are no friendly forces casualties.

Herat, 7.30 a.m.
A vehicle patrol from 207th ANA Corps strikes an IED in Adraskan District, killing three Afghan soldiers.

Ghazni, 8.05 a.m.

A US route clearance patrol strikes an IED in Wali Mohammed-E Shahid District. The explosion results in four US soldiers Cat A.

Kapisa, 8.55 a.m.

A joint foot patrol from 1st Kandak 3/201st ANA Corps, 202nd ANP Zone and 1er Régiment de Chasseurs Parachutistes (France) comes under small-arms fire in Tagab District. They positively identify the insurgent position and return fire. Forward Operating Base Kutshbach engages the insurgents with eight 120-mm rounds, forcing them to break contact. The attack results in the death of one French soldier.

Kandahar, 9.12 a.m.

A combined dismounted patrol from 1st Kandak 3/205th ANA Corps and 1st Squadron 32nd US Cavalry Regiment receives small-arms fire in Zharay District. They positively identify the insurgent firing position and return fire with small arms and 60-mm mortar rounds, forcing the insurgents to withdraw. Shortly afterwards, a 12-year-old Afghan civilian with a gunshot wound is brought to Combat Outpost Ahmed Khan and flown to Kandahar hospital, accompanied by his brother. The engagement results in two insurgents being killed (reported by village elders) and one insurgent wounded. The village elders state that they blame the insurgents for this incident and friendly forces have reported the potential use of Afghan civilians as human shields. The incident is under investigation. Friendly forces have initiated consequence management to include releasing a public-address message informing the public of insurgent use of Afghan civilians as human shields.

Khost, 10.03 a.m.

Afghan security forces at Border Security Point 1 in Terayzai District receive eleven 82-mm mortar rounds of insurgent indirect fire. The Afghan security forces positively identify a point of origin located inside Pakistan and conduct a counter-fire mission with nine 82-mm rounds. They also deploy a foot patrol to block an infiltration route from Pakistan. The patrol strikes an IED, killing three members of the Afghan security forces.

Wardak, 10.20 a.m.

A patrol from 202nd Afghan National Police Zone is engaged by an unknown number of insurgents with small-arms fire in Jalrayz District, leaving one police officer dead. Five insurgents are detained.

Logar, 10.30 a.m.

An insurgent with a vehicle-borne IED attempts to enter the Police Headquarters in Azrah District. After being denied entry, he drives to a nearby hospital and then detonates the device. This results in twenty Afghan civilians killed, twenty-three wounded and one insurgent killed. There are no ISAF forces on site. The President of Afghanistan and head of ISAF publicly condemn the attack.

Nahr-e Saraj, 1.15 p.m.

A vehicle in a mounted patrol from 215th ANA Corps strikes an IED containing around 20 kg of unknown bulk explosive charge in Nahr-e Saraj. The blast kills three ANA soldiers.

Kunar, 3.03 p.m.
A combined foot patrol from 2/201st ANA Corps and 2nd Battalion 35th US Infantry Regiment comes under small-arms and indirect fire from insurgents in Watahpur District. The patrol positively identifies the insurgents' position and returns fire. The engagement leaves one US soldier dead, four US soldiers Cat A, one US soldier Cat B, one Afghan soldier dead, one Afghan soldier Cat A, and two insurgents dead.

Helmand, 5.09 p.m.
While conducting a security operation in Nad-e Ali, 2nd Battalion 8th US Marines come under small-arms fire from insurgents. This results in one Marine Cat A (gunshot wound to right shoulder) and one Marine Cat B (gunshot wounds to the left foot and buttock). The Marines positively identify the insurgent firing position and return fire with small arms and a 40-mm grenade launcher. One round from the grenade launcher possibly lands short, resulting in two Marines Cat A (facial injuries). The wounded are flown back to Bastion in two missions (thirty-three minutes and forty-eight minutes). One of the Marines wounded by the 40-mm grenade goes into cardiac arrest at Bastion and dies. This is an unconfirmed blue-on-blue incident and is under investigation.

Nahr-e Saraj, 6.44 p.m.
Afghan police on a routine security operation 3.2 km north-east of Main Operating Base Price are caught in the blast from a suspected motorbike IED. It kills one policeman and wounds two others.

Kunar, 6.48 p.m.

A foot patrol from 2/201st ANA Corps comes under small-arms fire in Shigal Wa Sheltan District. Friendly forces positively identify the insurgents' position and return fire. Two A-10s from the 74th US Expeditionary Fighter Squadron drop three GBU-38 500-lb bombs on the insurgents' position. The initial firefight results in the death of one Afghan soldier.

Kunar, 10.30 p.m.

A US CH-47 (Chinook) crashes in Watahpur District, resulting in three US soldiers Cat A and three US soldiers Cat B. All twenty-four crew and passengers are recovered. The reason for the crash is under investigation, but it was not caused by insurgents.

Sunday 26th June 2011
Significant acts: 127

Helmand, 4.33 a.m.

A combined dismounted patrol from 2nd Kandak 2/215th ANA Corps and 1st Battalion 5th US Marines strikes an IED in Sangin. The blast results in one US Marine Cat A, one ANA soldier Cat A and one ANA soldier Cat B.

Helmand, 4.41 a.m.

A dismounted patrol from 1st Battalion 5th US Marines spends the night in a compound in Sangin after it has been swept twice – by engineers and an EOD team. They revert to 50% security for the night and remove their personal protective equipment. At first light, as they prepare to leave, one of the Marines triggers an IED, resulting in two Cat A (1 x double amputation, 1 x blown eardrum with bleeding from ears). They are flown back to Bastion in forty-seven minutes. No further casualties or damage are reported.

Paktika, 6.31 a.m.
A mounted patrol from 203rd ANA Corps strikes an IED in Bermal, killing three ANA.

Khost, 6.40 a.m.
A dismounted patrol from the Afghan security forces receives small-arms fire from an unknown number of insurgents in Tanai District. Border Security Point 4 Observation Post 2 positively identifies a point of origin located inside Pakistan and responds with an unknown number of 14.5-mm rounds, 40-mm grenades and 60-mm and 82-mm mortar rounds, forcing the insurgents to cease fire. Battle Damage Assessment is not conducted. There are no friendly casualties or damage reported. Task Force Duke (US) tries to notify the Pakistan Military Liaison Officer without success. The Khyber Border Coordination Centre is notified.

Helmand, 7.56 a.m.
A route clearance patrol from 2nd US Combat Engineer Battalion strikes an IED in Nahr-e Saraj. The blast results in one US Marine Cat A.

Helmand, 8.00 a.m.
A dismounted patrol from 3rd Battalion 4th US Marines receives small-arms fire from up to four insurgents in Nahr-e Saraj, resulting in one Marine Cat A (gunshot wound, lower back). Observation Post 22 positively identifies the insurgents' firing position and returns fire with small arms and eight 40-mm grenades. Patrol

Base Shark Tooth engages the insurgents with three 60-mm mortar rounds. While conducting the medevac mission, a HH-60 Pave Hawk helicopter receives small-arms fire but suffers no damage or injuries. An AH-1 Cobra attack helicopter fires twenty-one 2.75" rockets and five hundred 20-mm rounds on the insurgent positions, forcing them to cease fire. The wounded Marine is flown to Bastion in forty-eight minutes. Battle damage assessment is not conducted due to the tactical situation. There are no civilian casualties or damage reported.

Logar, 10.15 a.m.
A combined dismounted patrol from 1st Kandak 4/203rd ANA Corps and 2nd Battalion 30th US Infantry Regiment receives small-arms fire from insurgents in Charkh District. They positively identify the firing position and return fire, forcing the insurgents to break contact. The engagement results in one US soldier Cat A.

Helmand, 10.26 a.m.
A combined dismounted patrol from 2nd Kandak 2/215th ANA Corps and 1st Battalion 5th US Marines strikes an IED in Sangin District. The blast results in one Marine Cat A (partial double amputation). While securing a landing zone for the helicopter mede-vac, friendly forces strike another IED. This results in one Marine being killed. While friendly forces are waiting for the medevac helicopter to land, they observe an insurgent in the tree line with an AK-47. The insurgent engages them, and friendly forces return fire with an M249 light machine gun, wounding the insurgent, who takes cover behind a wall. Friendly forces then fire a 40-mm round from an M203 grenade launcher. All firing ceases. No battle damage assessment is conducted due to the tactical situation and

IED threat. An hour later, friendly forces strike a third IED, result-
ing in one Afghan soldier Cat A (left leg amputation).

Kandahar, 11.35 a.m.
A combined dismounted patrol from 1st Kandak 3/205th ANA
Corps and 1st Battalion 32nd US Infantry Regiment comes under
small-arms fire from two to three insurgents in Zharay District.
Friendly forces return fire, forcing them to break contact. The
engagement results in one US soldier Cat A.

Helmand, 11.49 a.m.
A mounted patrol from 3rd Battalion 4th US Marines strikes an
IED in Nahr-e Saraj. The blast results in two Marines Cat A (1 x
possible spinal injury, 1 x concussion) and one vehicle damaged.

Badghis, 12.21 p.m.
A mounted patrol from TF Badghis (Spain) strikes an IED in
Muqur District. The blast results in two Spanish soldiers being
killed, one Spanish soldier Cat A, one Spanish soldier Cat B, one
Spanish soldier Cat C and one vehicle damaged.

Helmand, 1.01 p.m.
A mounted patrol from Combat Logistics Battalion 8 (US) strikes
an IED in Washer District. The blast results in two US Marines
Cat A and one vehicle damaged.

Kandahar, 2.07 p.m.
A combined patrol from 2nd Kandak 3/205th ANA Corps and 4th
Squadron 4th US Cavalry Regiment is engaged by insurgent small-
arms and rocket-propelled grenade fire from multiple positions

at Combat Outpost Haji Rahmuddin in Zharay District. They positively identify the insurgents' positions and return fire. Two F/A-18Fs from US Carrier Air Wing 14 drop two 500-lb GBU-38 bombs on a building occupied by insurgents, forcing them to cease fire. The insurgent attack results in two ANA soldiers Cat A, and the air strike results in one building being destroyed. There are no civilian casualties reported.

Helmand, 2.15 p.m.

A mounted patrol from Combat Logistics Battalion 8 (US) strikes an IED in Washer District. The strike results in three US Marines Cat A and one vehicle damaged.

Ghazni, 5.10 p.m.

Soldiers from 2nd Battalion, 2nd US Infantry Regiment observe two individuals digging an IED into a road in Andar District. They declare them an imminent threat and fire three 120-mm and two 81-mm mortar rounds. Three Afghan civilians with minor shrapnel wounds later come to Forward Operating Base Andar, where they receive treatment. The incident is under investigation.

Kunar, 5.15 p.m.

A dismounted patrol from 2nd Battalion 35th US Infantry Regiment receives small-arms fire from insurgents in Shigal Wa Sheltan District. The attack results in one US soldier Cat A.

Helmand, 5.56 p.m.

Afghan police conducting a security operation at Patrol Base Amoo in Sangin receive small-arms fire and a rocket-propelled grenade, resulting in one policeman Cat B (fragmentation wound to right buttock). They respond with small-arms fire and five 60-mm mortar rounds. The insurgents break contact and leave the scene.

Helmand, 6.03 p.m.
A dismounted patrol from 42 Commando, Royal Marines strikes an IED on the Nahr-e Saraj/Nad-e Ali border, 500 metres from Check Point Toki. A US serviceman attached to the patrol is killed.

Helmand, 6.38 p.m.
ANP conducting a static security operation at Check Point Chaabak, 1.9 km north-west of Patrol Base 2 in Nahr-e Saraj, receive small-arms fire from insurgents, resulting in one ANP Cat A (sucking gunshot wound to the chest). Friendly forces observe a local national running south to north with what looks like a body in a wheelbarrow. They open fire but miss him. He hides between compounds and is not seen again.

Helmand, 6.40 p.m.
A combined dismounted patrol from 215th ANA Corps and 1st Battalion 5th US Marines is engaged by small-arms fire in Sangin. Friendly forces positively identify the firing position and return fire, killing one insurgent. Later a female Afghan civilian with Cat A wounds is taken to Forward Operating Base Sabit Qadam by her brother. She is flown to Bastion in forty-six minutes. Friendly forces speak to family and local elders about the incident and prepare radio messages emphasizing the insurgents' wilful endangerment of Afghan civilians.

Khost, 8.00 p.m.
Border Security Point 5 Observation Post 1 in Tanai District observes a suspicious insurgent vehicle at an historic firing position 1.6 km

inside Pakistan. An imminent threat is declared and the vehicle is engaged with three 60-mm mortar rounds. No battle damage assessment is conducted. The Pakistan Military Liaison Officer and Khyber Border Coordination Centre are notified.

Ghazni, 10.40 p.m.
A mounted patrol from Polish Battle Group Bravo strikes an IED in Qarah Bagh District. The blast results in two Polish soldiers Cat A and one logistics truck damaged.

APPENDIX 2

Afghanistan Fatality and Casualty Tables

NUMBER OF AFGHANISTAN UK MILITARY AND CIVILIAN FATALITIES
7th October 2001 to 31st December 2013

YEAR[1][2]	FATALITIES[3]			
	TOTAL	Killed in Action	Died of Wounds	Other[4]
TOTAL	447	353	51	43
2001	0	0	0	0
2002	3	0	0	3
2003	0	0	0	0
2004	1	1	0	0
2005	1	1	0	0
2006	39	20	1	18
2007	42	36	1	5
2008	51	47	3	1
2009	108	91	16	1
2010	103	80	15	8
2011	46	35	8	3
2012	44	35	5	4
2013	9	7	2	0

1. Data starts 7th October 2001.
2. The last three months of data are provisional and subject to change.
3. Some deaths may not have clearly defined cause information and could be subject to change depending on the outcome of Boards of Inquiry and/or Coroners' Inquest.
4. These data include all deaths occurring as a result of accidental or violent causes while deployed and deaths due to disease-related causes during the deployment.

NUMBER OF AFGHANISTAN UK MILITARY AND CIVILIAN CASUALTIES

7th October 2001 to 31st December 2013

YEAR[1][2]	CASUALTIES (Excl. Natural Causes)[3][4][5][6]			FIELD HOSPITAL ADMISSIONS[7][8][9]		
	TOTAL	Very Seriously Injured or Wounded	Seriously Injured or Wounded	TOTAL	Wounded in Action	Disease or Non-Battle Injury
TOTAL	610	303	307	7,186	2,171	5,015
2001	0	0	0			
2002	1	1	0			
2003	1	0	1			
2004	6	3	3			
2005	2	2	0			
2006	31	18	13	240	85	155
2007	63	23	40	832	234	598
2008	65	27	38	1,008	235	773
2009	157	82	75	1,229	508	721
2010	154	80	74	1,262	518	744
2011	69	34	35	921	274	647
2012	44	23	21	952	222	730
2013	17	10	7	742	95	647

1. Data starts 7th October 2001.
2. The last three months of data are provisional and subject to change.
3. The VSI and SI data includes personnel with an initial NOTICAS listing of VSI or SI who were alive at the time of discharge from their first hospital episode in the UK.
4. The VSI and SI injury data includes records classified as "Other Causes". This classification is used when there is insufficient information to attribute a casualty to injury or natural cause.
5. Civilians are not included in the figures previous to 1st January 2006.
6. The personnel listed as VSI or SI may also appear in the UK field-hospital admissions and aeromed evacuations data.
7. The admissions data contain UK personnel admitted to any field hospital, whether operated by UK or Coalition Medical Facilities.
8. The disease or non-battle injury figures are non-battle injuries only until 27th October 2006; disease is included from 28th October 2006 to be consistent with Op TELIC reporting.
9. Field Hospital Admissions data starts 1st March 2006.

MoD Definitions of "Very Seriously Injured" and "Seriously Injured"

The Notification of Casualty reports raised for casualties contain information on how serious medical staff in theatre judge their condition to be. This information is used to inform what the next of kin are told. "VSI" and "SI" are the two most serious categories into which personnel can be classified:

"Very Seriously Ill/Injured/Wounded" or VSI is the definition we use where the illness or injury is of such severity that life or reason is imminently endangered.

"Seriously Ill/Injured/Wounded" or SI is the definition we use where the patient's condition is of such severity that there is cause for immediate concern, but there is no imminent danger to life or reason.

The VSI and SI categories are defined by Joint Casualty and Compassionate Policy and Procedures. They are not strictly "medical categories" but are designed to give an indication of the severity of the illness to inform what the individual's next of kin are told. In the figures for Operation HERRICK (Afghanistan) and Operation TELIC (Iraq) we have excluded those individuals categorized as VSI or SI whose condition was identified to be caused by illness, to produce figures for the number of UK personnel categorized as VSI and SI whatever the cause of the injury, but excluding illnesses.

Glossary

ABP: Afghan Border Police
AH-64: Apache attack helicopter
ANA: Afghan National Army
ANP: Afghan National Police
ANSF: Afghan National Security Forces

Bergen: British Army rucksack
BFBS: British Forces Broadcasting Service
Brimstone: A counter-IED team made up of bomb-disposal experts
    and searchers. Also air-to-ground missiles used by RAF Tornados

DfID: Department for International Development

EOD: Explosive Ordnance Disposal

FOB: Forward Operating Base

Green Zone: The fertile land either side of the Helmand River

Hesco: Wire-mesh containers, lined with heavy-duty fabric and filled
    with rubble and hard core
Humvee: HMMWV – High Mobility Multi-Purpose Wheeled Vehicle

IDF: Indirect Fire, e.g. mortars, rockets, artillery
IED: Improvised Explosive Device
ISAF: International Security Assistance Force – the NATO-led security
    mission in Afghanistan
ISO Container: A steel freight container, usually forty feet long

JMOC: Joint Media Operations Centre

Mastiff: Armoured six-wheel patrol vehicle
MERT: Medical Emergency Response Team
MOG: Media Operations Group
MQ-1 Predator: Unmanned "aerial vehicle" – or "drone" – which can
    carry two Hellfire missiles
MQ-9 Reaper: The upgraded MQ-1 Predator
MTP: Multi Terrain Pattern – the army's new uniform, replacing the
    traditional green camouflage of DPM (Disruptive Pattern Material)

NAAFI: Navy, Army Air Force Institutes cafeteria and shop
NCO: Non-Commissioned Officer

OP: Observation Post
Osprey: Body armour worn by British soldiers

PB: Patrol Base
PRT: Provincial Reconstruction Team

REME: Royal Electrical and Mechanical Engineers
RPG: Rocket-Propelled Grenade
RSOI: Reception Staging and Onward Integration – induction training
    for all arrivals at Bastion

SA80: British Army's standard issue rifle
Shura: Afghan meeting, usually involving elders

TFH: Task Force Helmand

Vallon: Metal detector used in searching for IEDs

Acknowledgements

There are many friends and colleagues from the military and the BBC to whom I am indebted. First and foremost I want to thank Russ and Ali for allowing me to write about them. The same goes for Paul and Lee Swain. I would also like to thank Lt Col Crispin Lockhart, Lt Col Tim Purbrick, Lt Col Rosie Stone and Lt Col Vickie Sheriff.

I want to pay tribute to Mike McErlain, whose incredible work in the hospital at Camp Bastion saved the lives of so many injured servicemen and women. I also want to pay tribute to the fearless Ian Fisher.

From the BBC, I would like to thank all the ladies at Leicester, mostly for putting up with me for so long. Kate Squire, Kay Wright, Jane Hill, Lucy Collins, Lisa Hilliam, Kristina Hrywnak and Namrata Varia are all top of the list, along with all the other stalwarts in the newsroom.

At Alma Books I would like to thank Alex and Elisabetta for having so much faith in me, and Christian Müller for putting up with all my titivations.

Of my old friends to whom I must tip my hat: Colly and Ghillie, both for their willingness to drink with me, Eddie for all the legal shenanigans and Jamie, Dave and Bushy for joining me up the mountain. Special thanks must also go to my old mate Tucker, for absorbing and deflecting so many years of really bad poetry.

I'd like to mention – and thank – all the dogs that have kept me fit and brought me so much happiness throughout my life. In no particular order: Jasper, Monty, Trudie, Hector, Nelson, Nelly, Tess, Katja and Tanya.

Above all else, I am grateful to my mother and father for all their help and encouragement throughout my years. I must also mention my brother Will and my sister Nicky for their ongoing support, along with my beautiful girlfriend Belinda.